English Language Arts
Activity Book

4

Book Staff and Contributors

Kristen Kinney-Haines   *Director, English Language Arts*
Amy Rauen   *Director, Instructional Design*
Mary Beck Desmond   *Senior Text Editor*
Allyson Jacob   *Text Editor*
Tricia Battipede   *Senior Creative Manager*
Julie Jankowski   *Senior Visual Designer*
Caitlin Gildrien   *Visual Designer*
Sheila Smith   *Print Designer*
Tricia Battipede, Mike Bohman, Shannon Palmer   *Cover Designers*
Robyn Campbell, Heather Evans, Alane Gernon-Paulsen, Tara Gleason, Tim Mansfield, Melisa Rice,
       Tisha Ruibal   *Writers*
Amy Eward   *Content Specialist; Senior Manager, Writers and Editors*
Dan Smith   *Senior Project Manager*

Doug McCollum   *Senior Vice President, Product Development*
Kristin Morrison   *Vice President, Design, Creative, and User Experience*
Rohit Lakhani   *Vice President, Program Management and Operations*
Kelly Engel   *Senior Director, Curriculum*
Christopher Frescholtz   *Senior Director, Program Management*
Erica Castle   *Director, Creative Services*
Lisa Dimaio Iekel   *Senior Production Manager*

Illustrations Credits

All illustrations © Stride, Inc. unless otherwise noted
Characters: Tommy DiGiovanni, Matt Fedor, Ben Gamache, Shannon Palmer
Cover: Crane © Bennyartist/Shutterstock; Spiral © Silmen/iStock

At Stride, Inc. (NYSE: LRN)—formerly K12 Inc.—we are reimagining lifelong learning as a rich, deeply personal experience that prepares learners for tomorrow. Since its inception, Stride has been committed to removing barriers that impact academic equity and to providing high-quality education for anyone—particularly those in underserved communities. The company has transformed the teaching and learning experience for millions of people by providing innovative, high-quality, tech-enabled education solutions, curriculum, and programs directly to students, schools, the military, and enterprises in primary, secondary, and post-secondary settings. Stride is a premier provider of K-12 education for students, schools, and districts, including career learning services through middle and high school curriculum. Providing a solution to the widening skills gap in the workplace and student loan crisis, Stride equips students with real world skills for in-demand jobs with career learning. For adult learners, Stride delivers professional skills training in healthcare and technology, as well as staffing and talent development for Fortune 500 companies. Stride has delivered millions of courses over the past decade and serves learners in all 50 states and more than 100 countries. The company is a proud sponsor of the Future of School, a nonprofit organization dedicated to closing the gap between the pace of technology and the pace of change in education. More information can be found at stridelearning.com, K12.com, destinationsacademy.com, galvanize.com, techelevator.com, and medcerts.com.

ISBN: 978-1-60153-573-3

Printed by Walsworth, Saint Joseph, MI, USA, May 2021.

Table of Contents

Emoji and Pisa and Birds, Oh My!

Mystery!

Frontiers of Flight

Childhood Classics

Choice Reading Project

Men and Women of Character

Healthy and Safe

Cinderella Around the World (A)

Spelling List 1 Pretest

1. Open the Spelling Pretest activity online. Listen to the first spelling word. Type the word. Check your answer.

2. Write the correct spelling of the word in the Word column of the Spelling Pretest table on the next page.

Word	✓	✗
1 blindfold		

3. Put a check mark in the ✓ column if you spelled the word correctly online.

Word	✓	✗
1 blindfold	✓	

Put an X in the ✗ column if you spelled the word incorrectly online.

Word	✓	✗
1 blindfold		X

4. Repeat Steps 1–3 for the remaining words in the Spelling Pretest.

Cinderella Around the World (A)

Spelling List 1 Pretest

Write each spelling word in the Word column, making sure to spell it correctly.

	Word	✓	✗
1			
2			
3			
4			
5			
6			
7			
8			
9			
10			
11			
12			
13			

	Word	✓	✗
14			
15			
16			
17			
18			
19			
20			
21			
22			
23			
24			
25			

Cinderella Around the World (A)

Write About Theme

Read the passage from *Yeh-Shen: A Cinderella Story from China* retold by Ai-Ling Louie. Then answer the questions in complete sentences.

The old man sighed and said, "Yes, my child, your fish is no longer alive, and I must tell you that your stepmother is once more the cause of your sorrow." Yeh-Shen gasped in horror, but the old man went on. "Let us not dwell on things that are past," he said, "for I have come bringing you a gift. Now you must listen carefully to this: The bones of your fish are filled with a powerful spirit. Whenever you are in serious need, you must kneel before them and let them know your heart's desire. But do not waste their gifts."

1. To determine the themes of a story, readers must consider the characters' actions.

   a. Based on the passage, what word best describes the actions of Yeh-Shen's stepmother? Identify a sentence from the passage that supports your answer.

   _____

   _____

   _____

   _____

b. What lesson might readers learn from the stepmother's actions?

_____

_____

_____

_____

_____

2. A theme is a message an author wants to share with readers. It is something the author wants readers to learn about life.

   a. What is one of the themes of _Yeh-Shen: A Cinderella Story from China_?

   _____

   _____

   _____

   _____

   _____

   b. What evidence from the text supports this theme?

   _____

   _____

   _____

   _____

   _____

Cinderella Around the World (B)

Spelling List 1 Activity Bank

Circle any words in the box that you did not spell correctly on the pretest. Using your circled words, complete one activity of your choice. Complete as much of the activity as you can in the time given.

If you spelled all words correctly on the pretest, complete your chosen activity with as many spelling words as you can.

album	optimist	system	magnetism	people
establishment	planet	witness	magnetize	rewind
admit	subject	contest	Connecticut	renew
insect	absent	magnet	Wisconsin	replace
object	habitat	magnetic	could	revise

Spelling Activity Choices

Vowel-Free Words

1. In the left column, write only the consonants in each word and put a dot where each vowel should be.

2. Spell each word out loud, stating which vowels should be in the places you wrote dots.

3. In the right column, rewrite the entire spelling word.

4. Correct any spelling errors.

Alphabetizing

1. In the left column, write your words from the spelling word list in alphabetical order.

2. Correct any spelling errors.

Rhymes

1. In the left column, write your words from the spelling word list.

2. In the right column, write a rhyming word for each of your spelling words.

3. Correct any spelling errors.

Uppercase and Lowercase

1. In the left column, write each of your words in all capital letters, or all uppercase.

2. In the right column, write each of your words in all lowercase letters.

3. Correct any spelling errors.

Complete the activity that you chose.

My chosen activity: _____

1. _____ _____
2. _____ _____
3. _____ _____
4. _____ _____
5. _____ _____
6. _____ _____
7. _____ _____
8. _____ _____
9. _____ _____
10. _____ _____
11. _____ _____
12. _____ _____
13. _____ _____
14. _____ _____
15. _____ _____
16. _____ _____
17. _____ _____
18. _____ _____
19. _____ _____
20. _____ _____
21. _____ _____
22. _____ _____
23. _____ _____
24. _____ _____
25. _____ _____

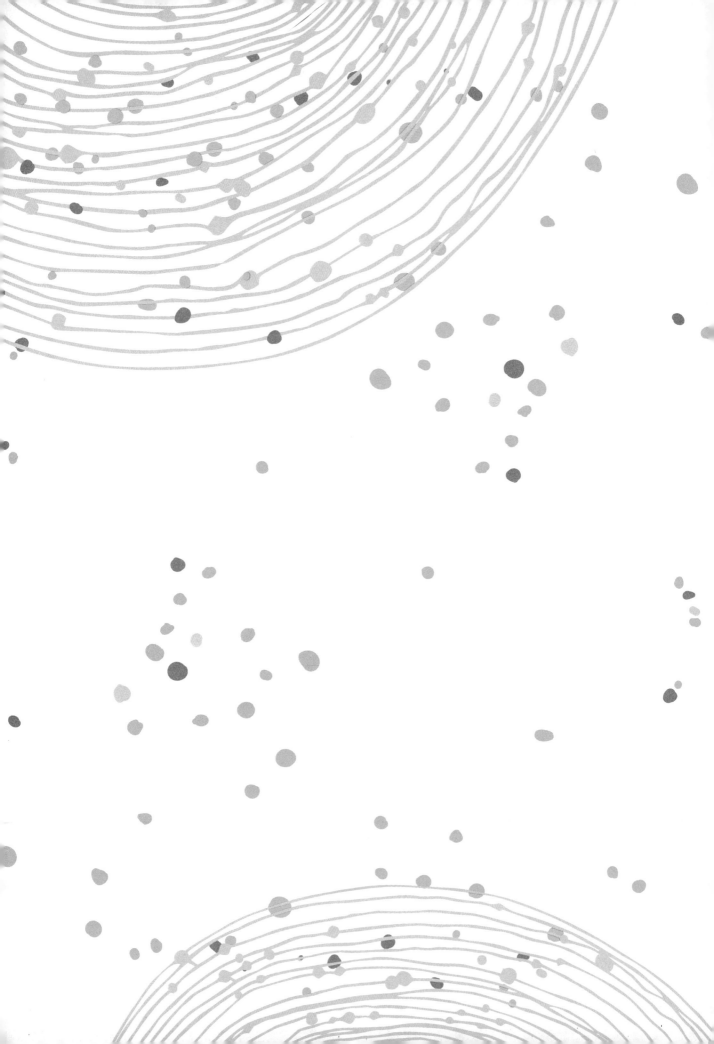

Cinderella Around the World (B)

Prepare to Write a Summary of *Adelita*

Write your responses in complete sentences.

1. A summary of a story should include only the most important details and events. Those details include the main characters and the setting.

   a. Who are the main characters in *Adelita*?

   _____

   _____

   b. What is the setting of the story?

   _____

   _____

2. A summary should include the most important events from the beginning, middle, and end of a story.

   a. What are the most important events from the beginning of the story?

   _____

   _____

   _____

   _____

b. What are the most important events from the middle of the story?

_____

_____

_____

_____

_____

_____

_____

c. What are the most important events from the end of the story?

_____

_____

_____

_____

3. Characters often have problems that must be solved. Details about the problem and how it is solved should be included in a summary.

a. What are Adelita's problems?

_____

_____

_____

_____

b. How are Adelita's problems solved? Who helps her solve them?

_____

_____

_____

_____

4. A summary should include big ideas or themes from the story. What is one possible theme in _Adelita_? What evidence from the story supports this theme?

_____

_____

_____

_____

_____

_____

_____

_____

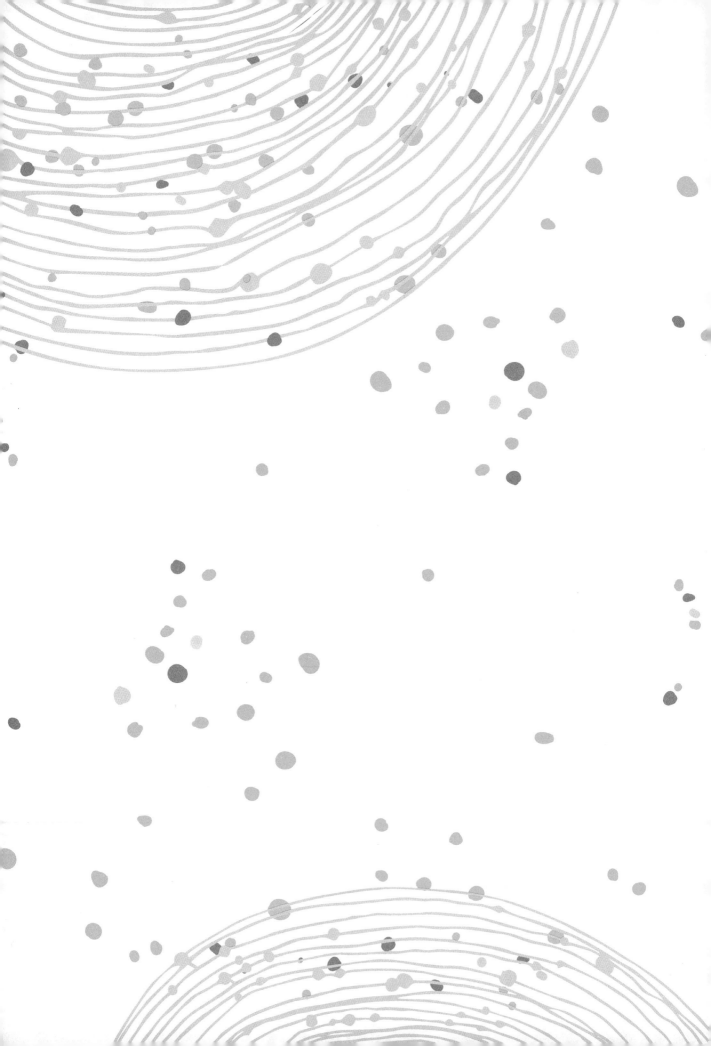

Cinderella Around the World (C)

Write a Summary of "Cinderella"

Write your response in complete sentences.

Write a one-page summary of "Cinderella." Be sure to include the following:

- Main characters
- Setting
- Most important events from the beginning, middle, and end of the story
- Problems the characters face and how they solve those problems

Remember that your summary should include only key details and important ideas or themes.

_____

_____

_____

_____

_____

_____

_____

_____

_____

_____

_____

_____

_____

TRY IT

Cinderella Around the World (D)

Write About Inferences

Read the passage from *Glass Slipper, Gold Sandal* by Paul Fleischman.
Then answer the questions in complete sentences.

> All night the girl danced with the headman's son, until the first rooster crowed. Then she remembered—she had to leave at once.

1. What can you infer that the girl's magical helper told her before she went to the ball?

    _____

    _____

    _____

    _____

2. What information from your background knowledge helped you to make the inference about what the magical helper told the girl?

    _____

    _____

    _____

    _____

3. What clues in the text helped you make the inference about what the magical helper told the girl? How did those clues help you?

_____

_____

_____

_____

_____

_____

You don't need a magical helper to make inferences. Just look for clues!

Cinderella Around the World (E)

Compare Cinderella Stories

Complete the comparison chart with details from each of the Cinderella stories listed.

Title	*Yeh-Shen*	*Adelita*	"Cinderella"
Main Characters			
What is the Cinderella character like?			
Setting			
How does Cinderella end up with a stepmother?			

Title	Yeh-Shen	Adelita	"Cinderella"
Who helps Cinderella? What special items does Cinderella get?			
What is the special event? What is the reason for the special event?			
How is Cinderella's identity revealed?			
How does the story end?			
What is one theme (big idea) of the story?			

Cinderella Around the World Wrap-Up

Write About Cinderella Stories

Write your responses in complete sentences.

Choose two of these Cinderella stories to compare: *Yeh-Shen*, *Adelita*, and "Cinderella." Answer the following questions to compare the two stories you choose. Be sure to include key details from both stories to support your points.

1. Setting: How are the time and place in which the stories are set the same and different?

_____

_____

_____

_____

2. Characters: Who are the main characters in each story and what are they like?

_____

_____

_____

_____

_____

_____

3. Events: How are the events of the two stories alike, and how are they different? Be sure to describe each story's ending.

_____

_____

_____

_____

_____

_____

_____

_____

_____

_____

_____

_____

4. Theme: What is a big idea from each story? How do the events and ending support those themes?

_____

_____

_____

_____

_____

_____

Narrative Writing Skills (A)

Spelling List 2 Pretest

1. Open the Spelling Pretest activity online. Listen to the first spelling word. Type the word. Check your answer.

2. Write the correct spelling of the word in the Word column of the Spelling Pretest table on the next page.

Word	✓	✗
1 blindfold		

3. Put a check mark in the ✓ column if you spelled the word correctly online.

Word	✓	✗
1 blindfold	✓	

Put an X in the ✗ column if you spelled the word incorrectly online.

Word	✓	✗
1 blindfold		✗

4. Repeat Steps 1–3 for the remaining words in the Spelling Pretest.

Narrative Writing Skills (A)

Spelling List 2 Pretest

Write each spelling word in the Word column, making sure to spell it correctly.

	Word	✓	✗
1			
2			
3			
4			
5			
6			
7			
8			
9			

	Word	✓	✗
10			
11			
12			
13			
14			
15			
16			
17			

TRY IT

Narrative Writing Skills (A)

The Story of an Object

Use the story prompt to answer the questions.

Story prompt: **Write a story narrated by . . . an object!** Have the object describe an experience it had. For example, a coin might describe its journey from a piggy bank to the drawer of a cash register.

1. Think about your story.

   a. Who will narrate the story?

   _____

   b. Good writers think about audience. Who do you imagine reading the story?

   _____

   c. What other characters will be in the story? Describe at least one character.

   _____

   _____

   d. Where is the story set? Give some details about the time and place of the story.

   _____

   _____

2. Write an introduction to your story. You should introduce the narrator, the setting, and the situation (or point). If you choose, introduce other characters. Imagine that you're writing to your audience.

_____

_____

_____

_____

_____

_____

Now I am starting to feel bad about tossing my sweatshirt into a pile of dirty laundry....

3. What happens next? Complete the diagram to describe how your story will be organized. **(Do not write the whole story now. Just describe what will happen.)**

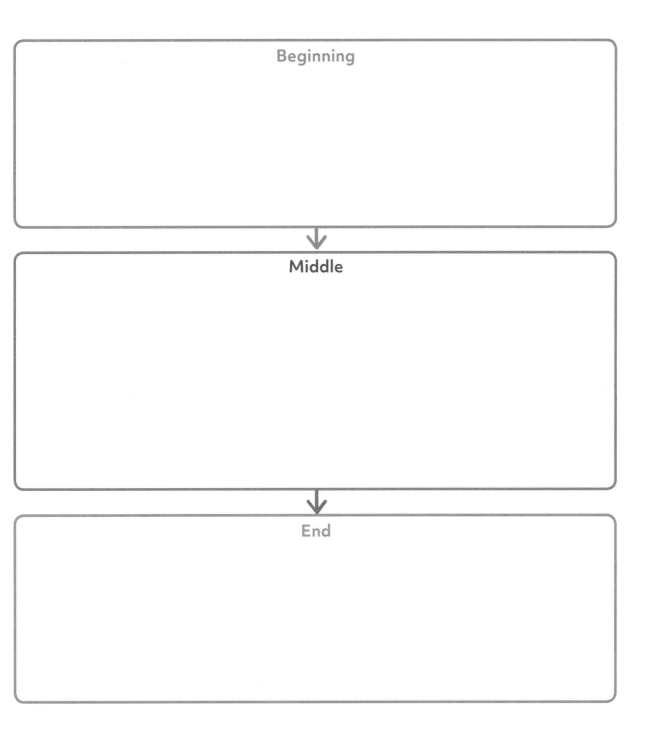

Beginning

Middle

End

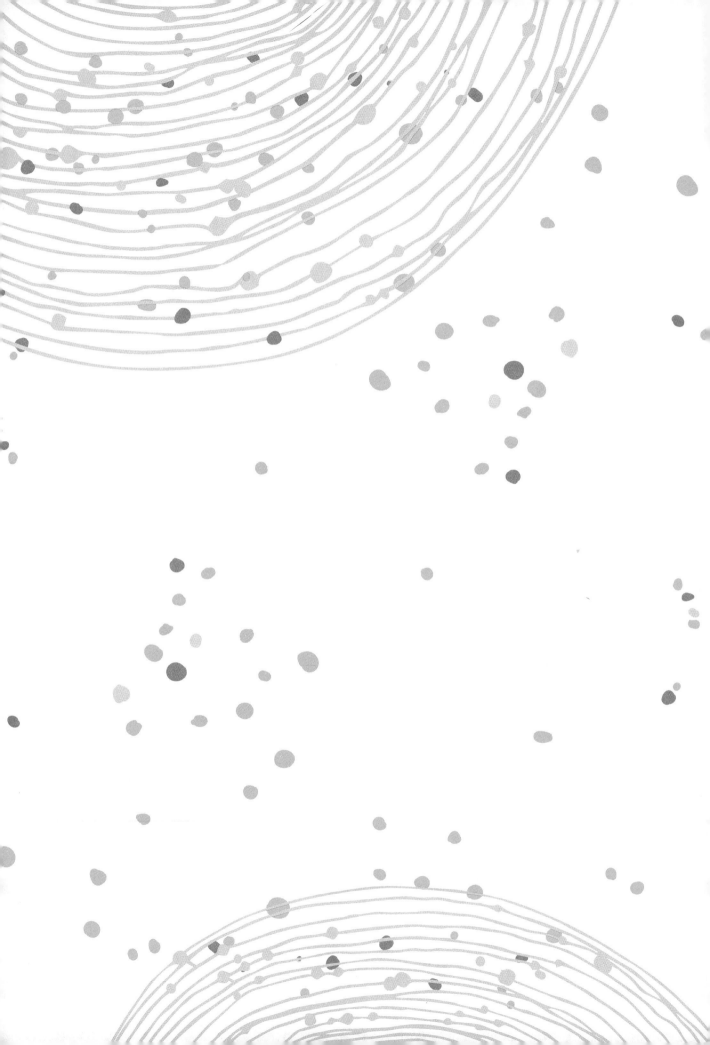

Narrative Writing Skills (B)

Spelling List 2 Activity Bank

Circle any words in the box that you did not spell correctly on the pretest. Using your circled words, complete one activity of your choice. Complete as much of the activity as you can in the time given.

If you spelled all words correctly on the pretest, complete your chosen activity with as many spelling words as you can.

blender	smashed	creation	Ohio	unaware
fixing	splitting	creativity	unlucky	uncommon
jammed	stepped	Kansas	unplug	unknown
slugger	create			

Spelling Activity Choices

Silly Sentences

1. Write a silly sentence using your words from the spelling word list.

2. Underline the spelling word in each sentence.
   Example: The dog was <u>driving</u> a car.

3. Correct any spelling errors.

Spelling Story

1. Write a very short story using your words from the spelling word list.

2. Underline the spelling words in the story.

3. Correct any spelling errors.

Riddle Me This

1. Write a riddle for your words from the spelling word list.
   Example: "I have a trunk, but it's not on my car."

2. Write the answer, which is your word, for each riddle.
   Example: Answer: elephant

3. Correct any spelling errors.

RunOnWord

1. Gather some crayons, colored pencils, or markers. Write each of your words, using a different color for each word, end to end as one long word.
   Example: dogcatbirdfishturtle

2. Rewrite the words correctly and with proper spacing.

Complete the activity that you chose.

My chosen activity: _____

_____

_____

_____

_____

_____

_____

_____

_____

_____

_____

_____

_____

_____

_____

_____

_____

_____

_____

_____

_____

_____

_____

_____

_____

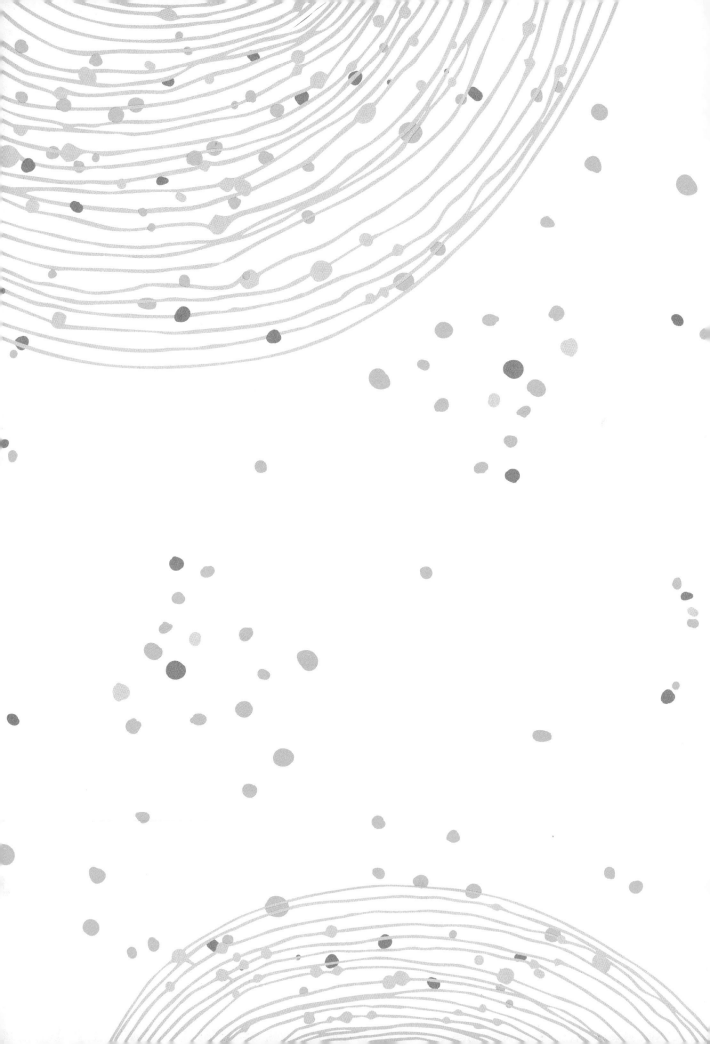

Narrative Writing Skills (B)

Use Your Best Words

Use the story prompt to answer the questions.

Story prompt: **Write a story narrated by . . . an object!** Have the object describe an experience it had. For example, a coin might describe its journey from a piggy bank to the drawer of a cash register.

1. Write the middle of your story. Start by writing about the problem that your object faces. Write until the problem is *almost* solved. Remember, *show* the events in your story—don't just tell about them.

_____

_____

_____

_____

_____

_____

_____

_____

_____

_____

_____

_____

2. Transitions help show the sequence of events.

   a. Did you use a transition in your response to Question 1? If yes, circle it.
      If you didn't use a transition, revise a sentence to include a transition.

      Original sentence:

      _____

      Revised sentence:

      _____

   b. Explain how your transition helps show the sequence of events.

      _____

      _____

3. Concrete language and sensory details help show exactly what's
   happening in a story.

   a. Underline your two strongest sensory details in your response to
      Question 1. Explain why you chose those details.

      _____

      _____

   b. Put a box around one detail that could be stronger. Maybe it is
      abstract. Maybe it does not use sensory language. Revise that detail.

      Original detail:

      _____

      Revised detail:

      _____

Finish Your Story

Use the story prompt to answer the questions.

Story prompt: **Write a story narrated by . . . an object!** Have the object describe an experience it had. For example, a coin might describe its journey from a piggy bank to the drawer of a cash register.

1. Draw a picture of something that happens at the end of your story.

a. Write one or two sentences that describe what is happening in the picture. Do not use the verb *to be* in your sentence.

b. What does your sentence show readers about the narrator or characters?

_____

_____

c. What does your sentence show readers about what is happening?

_____

_____

2. Dialogue also shows what happens and how characters respond to events.

a. Write dialogue between the narrator and another character.

Narrator's name	Character's name

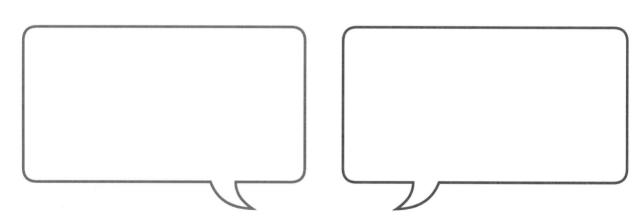

b. What does the dialogue show readers about the narrator and character?

_____

_____

c. What does the dialogue show readers about what is happening?

_____

_____

3. Write the conclusion of your story.

_____

_____

_____

_____

_____

_____

_____

That's a wrap! Everybody—
and everything—truly has
a story to tell.

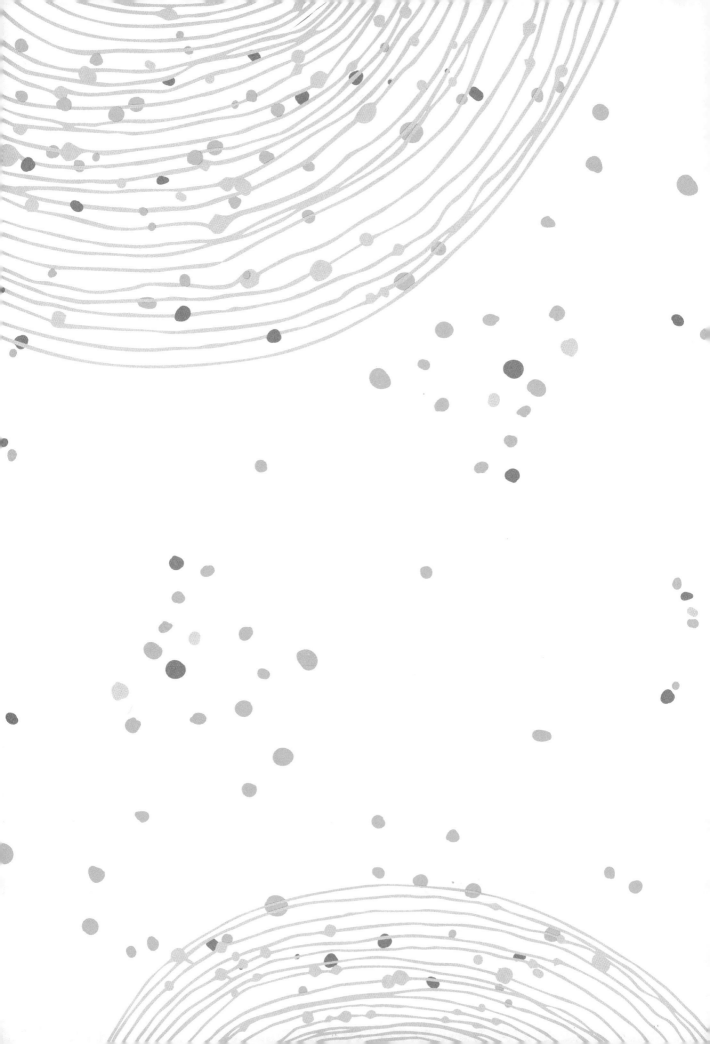

Narrative Writing Skills Wrap-Up

Use Narrative Writing Skills

Use the picture prompt to answer the questions.

1. The scene in the picture is part of a narrative. Write a short introduction to this narrative.

_____

_____

_____

_____

    a. In your introduction, circle the words that reveal who the narrator is. (If necessary, add or revise text to reveal the narrator.)

    b. In your introduction, underline the words that reveal what the situation is. (If necessary, add or revise text to reveal the situation.)

2. Use sensory language to describe the picture. For some of the senses, use your imagination. For example, how do you think the farm smells? What flavor could the ice cream be? For each sense, write at least one word or phrase.

a. sight: _____

b. smell: _____

c. hearing: _____

d. taste: _____

e. touch: _____

3. Write dialogue between two characters in the picture. Explain what your dialogue reveals about the characters.

Character's name   Character's name

What dialogue reveals:

_____

_____

4. The picture could show something happening at any point in a story. Describe the beginning, middle, and end of a story that includes the scene in the picture.

5. Think about your idea for a conclusion in Question 4. Explain why this conclusion is logical.

_____

_____

6. Read these sentences:

- Ben licked his ice cream cone.

- A chicken darted toward him and snatched the cone.

a. You can use a transition to connect the ideas. What transition would you add to the beginning of the second sentence?

_____

b. Explain how the transition affects the meaning of the sentences.

_____

_____

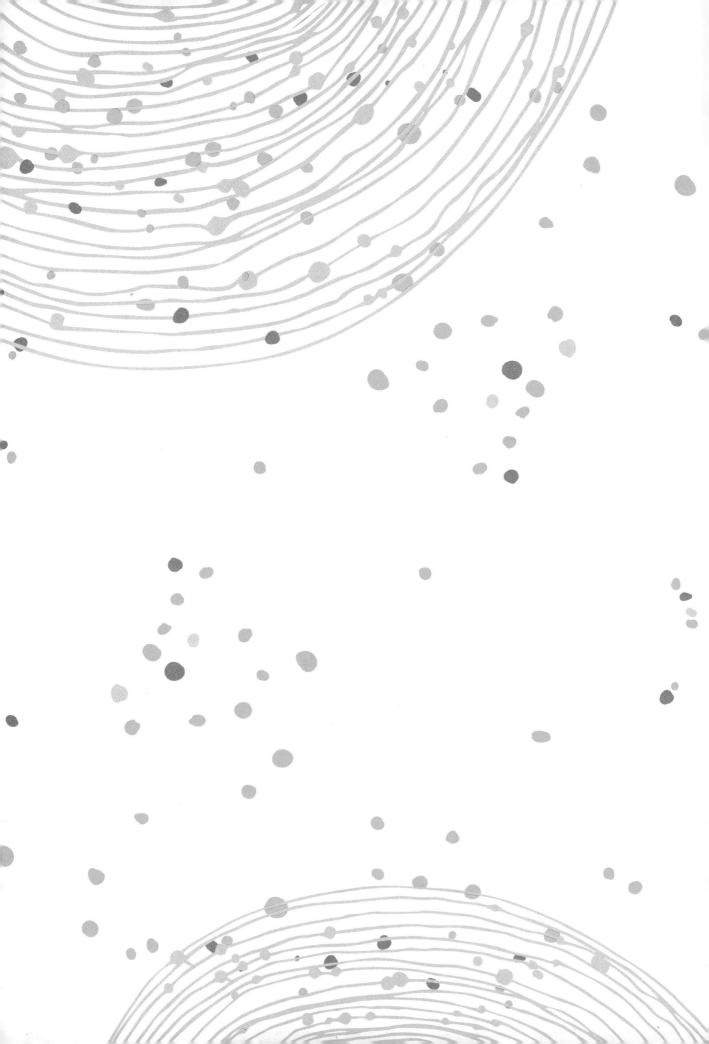

Word Relationships

Apply: Word Relationships

Use a dictionary or thesaurus to find synonyms and/or antonyms for each vocabulary word.

1. **infer**

   synonyms: _____

2. **integrate**

   synonyms: _____

   antonyms: _____

3. **interpret**

   synonyms: _____

4. **paraphrase**

   synonyms: _____

   antonyms: _____

5. **summarize**

   synonyms: _____

   antonyms: _____

6. **evidence**

   synonyms: _____

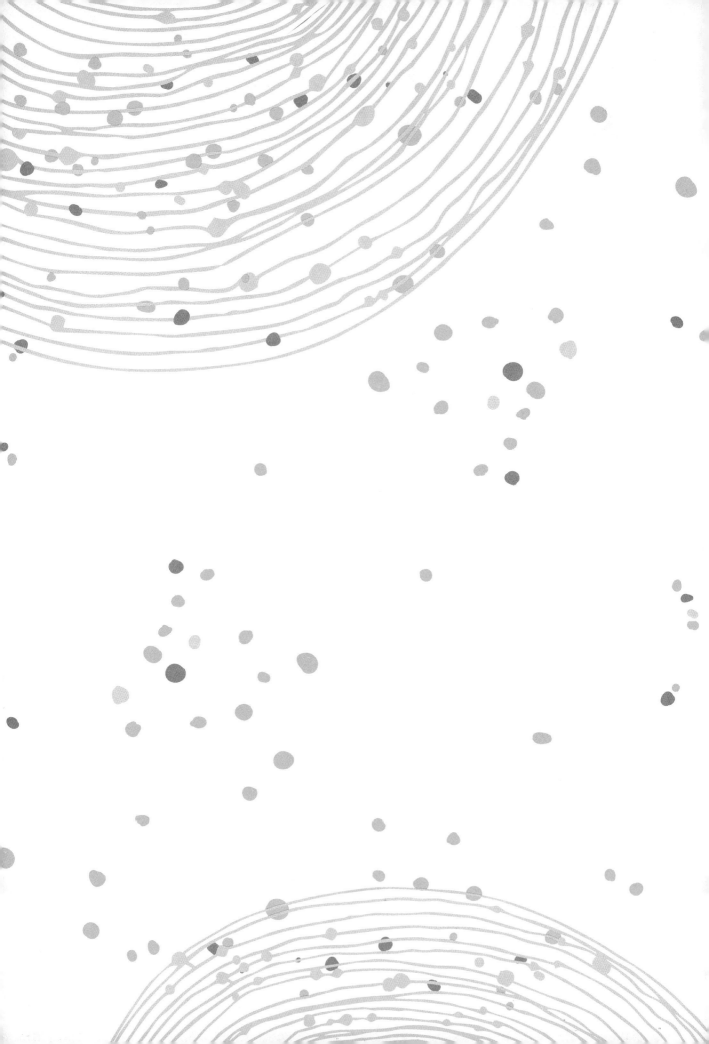

"From Cave Paintings to Emoji"

Spelling List 3 Pretest

1. Open the Spelling Pretest activity online. Listen to the first spelling word. Type the word. Check your answer.

2. Write the correct spelling of the word in the Word column of the Spelling Pretest table on the next page.

Word	✓	✗
1 blindfold		

3. Put a check mark in the ✓ column if you spelled the word correctly online.

Word	✓	✗
1 blindfold	✓	

Put an X in the ✗ column if you spelled the word incorrectly online.

Word	✓	✗
1 blindfold		X

4. Repeat Steps 1–3 for the remaining words in the Spelling Pretest.

"From Cave Paintings to Emoji"

Spelling List 3 Pretest

Write each spelling word in the Word column, making sure to spell it correctly.

	Word	✓	✗
1			
2			
3			
4			
5			
6			
7			
8			
9			

	Word	✓	✗
10			
11			
12			
13			
14			
15			
16			
17			

"From Cave Paintings to Emoji"

Paraphrase Using a Time Line

Good readers use text features to help them understand the information in a text. In "From Cave Paintings to Emoji," the author uses a time line to display the key events of the history of human communication.

1. Using the information provided in the time line, paraphrase the events of human communication from 1969 to 2015.

Original Information	Paraphrase
1999—The first emoji begin appearing on mobile phones in Japan. 2015—Emoji become increasingly popular as more and more phone systems include them.	
1977—Apple introduces the Apple II personal computer. 1984—Motorola introduces the first handheld cell phone. 2007—Apple introduces the iPhone.	

2. On page 17, in the first paragraph of the section "Express Yourself," you learn information about emoji. What additional information did you learn about emoji from the time line?

_____

_____

_____

_____

3. As a reader, you learned more information about emoji from the time line. Next time you see a time line or another text feature, what will you do and why?

_____

_____

_____

_____

"From Cave Paintings to Emoji" Wrap-Up

Spelling List 3 Activity Bank

Circle any words in the box that you did not spell correctly on the pretest. Using your circled words, complete one activity of your choice. Complete as much of the activity as you can in the time given.

If you spelled all words correctly on the pretest, complete your chosen activity with as many spelling words as you can.

buzzes	glasses	recommends	Arkansas	rough
connects	infants	interact	New Hampshire	disagree
crunches	invents	react	enough	disappear
diminishes	mixes			

Spelling Activity Choices

Hidden Words

1. Draw a picture and "hide" as many words from the Spelling Word List inside the picture as you can.

2. See if others can find the words within the picture.

Triangle Spelling

Write each word in a triangle.

Ghost Words

1. Use a white crayon to write each spelling word.

2. Go over the white crayon writing with a colored marker.

Complete the activity that you chose.

My chosen activity: _____

"From Cave Paintings to Emoji" Wrap-Up

Paraphrasing Modern Human Communication

Paraphrasing is important because it shows that you really understand the information in a text.

Paraphrase the information you learned from the text on page 15 of the article in the section called Computers and the Internet. Be sure to include information you learned from text features, such as captions.

Details from Text	Paraphrase

Use ideas you paraphrased in the table to write a paragraph.

_____

_____

_____

_____

_____

_____

I'm holding the "computer" that I use most often!

"Counterfeit Money: Then and Now"

Compare and Contrast

Authors use text features and the structure of informational texts to help readers navigate and learn more information. Use the articles "From Cave Paintings to Emoji" and "Counterfeit Money: Then and Now" to answer the questions.

1. Compare and contrast the information from the time lines in both articles.

    a. Describe the first and last events on the time line from the article "From Cave Paintings to Emoji."

    _____

    _____

    _____

    _____

    b. Describe the first and last events on the time line from the article "Counterfeit Money: Then and Now."

    _____

    _____

    _____

    _____

    c. What is the same about the information you learned from the time lines? What is different?

    _____

    _____

2. Both articles use other text features to teach more information. Look at the bar graph on page 17. What information does this text feature show you, and what does it help you to understand?

_____

_____

_____

3. The articles use different organizational structures. One uses time order (sequential) and the other uses compare and contrast. Use your knowledge of both structures to fill in the blanks.

a. The organizational structure in "From Cave Paintings to Emoji" is

_____

_____

I know this because

_____

_____

_____

How does this structure help the reader?

_____

_____

_____

b. The organizational structure in "Counterfeit Money: Then and Now" is

_____

_____

I know this because

_____

_____

_____

How does this structure help the reader?

_____

_____

_____

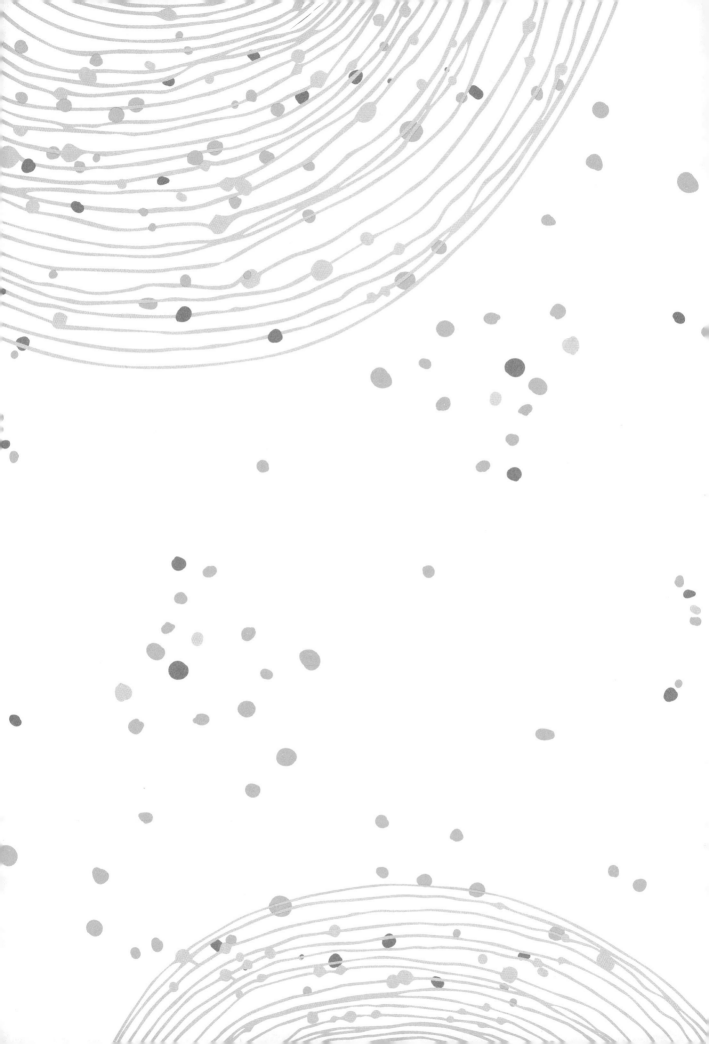

"Counterfeit Money: Then and Now" Wrap-Up

Compare and Contrast Information

Turn to the section Fake vs. Real on pages 46–47 in the article "Counterfeit Money: Then and Now." Reread these two pages.

1. Make notes in the table about what you learned about counterfeit money detection today and long ago.

Today	Long Ago

2. Compare: What is the same about counterfeit money detection today and in the past?

_____

_____

_____

_____

_____

_____

3. Contrast: What is different about counterfeit money dectection today from what it was like in the past?

_____

_____

_____

_____

_____

Narrative Writing: Prewriting (A)

Spelling List 4 Pretest

1. Open the Spelling Pretest activity online. Listen to the first spelling word. Type the word. Check your answer.

2. Write the correct spelling of the word in the Word column of the Spelling Pretest table on the next page.

Word	✓	✗
1 blindfold		

3. Put a check mark in the ✓ column if you spelled the word correctly online.

Word	✓	✗
1 blindfold	✓	

Put an X in the ✗ column if you spelled the word incorrectly online.

Word	✓	✗
1 blindfold		X

4. Repeat Steps 1–3 for the remaining words in the Spelling Pretest.

Narrative Writing: Prewriting (A)

Spelling List 4 Pretest

Write each spelling word in the Word column, making sure to spell it correctly.

	Word	✓	✗
1			
2			
3			
4			
5			
6			
7			
8			
9			

	Word	✓	✗
10			
11			
12			
13			
14			
15			
16			
17			

Narrative Writing: Prewriting (A)

Brainstorm for Your Personal Narrative

Read the writing assignment.

Prompt: **Write about a meaningful moment in your life.**

Requirements: Your narrative should have the following:

- A **title**

- A logical sequence, including an **introduction, body,** and **conclusion**

- A well-developed **narrator** and at least one other **character**, as well as a clear **situation** (setting and necessary background information)

- **Dialogue** and **description** that develop events and show how characters respond to situations

- **Sensory language**, including **imagery**

- **Transitions** that show sequence

- Correct **grammar, usage,** and **mechanics**

Audience: Your teacher and peers

Purpose: Show readers why the experience was meaningful.

Length: 300–400 words long, approximately 4–6 handwritten drafting pages or $1-1\frac{1}{2}$ pages typed and double spaced

Brainstorm and choose a topic for your personal narrative.

1. List as many possible topics as you can think of.

    _____   _____

    _____   _____

    _____   _____

    _____   _____

    _____   _____

    _____   _____

2. Read your list of topics. Circle any topics that you really would like to write about. If you didn't circle any topics, add a few more to your list.

3. Choose your favorite topic that you circled. Then answer Yes or No to each question.

    a. Is the topic small enough to describe in detail in just a few pages? _____

    b. Is the topic something you can *show* with description, dialogue, and sensory words? _____

    c. Is the topic meaningful to you? _____

4. Did you answer Yes to Parts A–C of Question 3? You have found a topic! If not, go back and complete Question 3 with another topic from your list. Repeat until you find a topic that works.

My personal narrative topic is

_____

Narrative Writing: Prewriting (B)

Spelling List 4 Activity Bank

Circle any words in the box that you did not spell correctly on the pretest. Using your circled words, complete one activity of your choice. Complete as much of the activity as you can in the time given.

If you spelled all words correctly on the pretest, complete your chosen activity with as many spelling words as you can.

bacon	exhale	sustain	transport	precaution
danger	fragrant	waiting	Delaware	prehistoric
erase	layer	portable	Maine	preview
essay	scale			

Spelling Activity Choices

Create a Crossword

1. Write a word from your spelling word list in the center of the grid paper.

2. Write another spelling word going across and sharing a letter with the first word. See how many words you can connect.

   Example:

			p			
		k	i	s	s	e	s
	d		n			
r	o	c	k	s		
	g					
	s					

Word Search Puzzle

1. Draw a box on the grid paper. The box should be large enough to hold your words from the spelling word list.

2. Fill in the grid paper with words from your spelling list, writing them horizontally, vertically, and diagonally (forwards or backwards if you choose).

3. Fill in the rest of the box with random letters.

4. Ask someone to find and circle your spelling words in the puzzle you made.

Complete the activity that you chose.

My chosen activity: _____

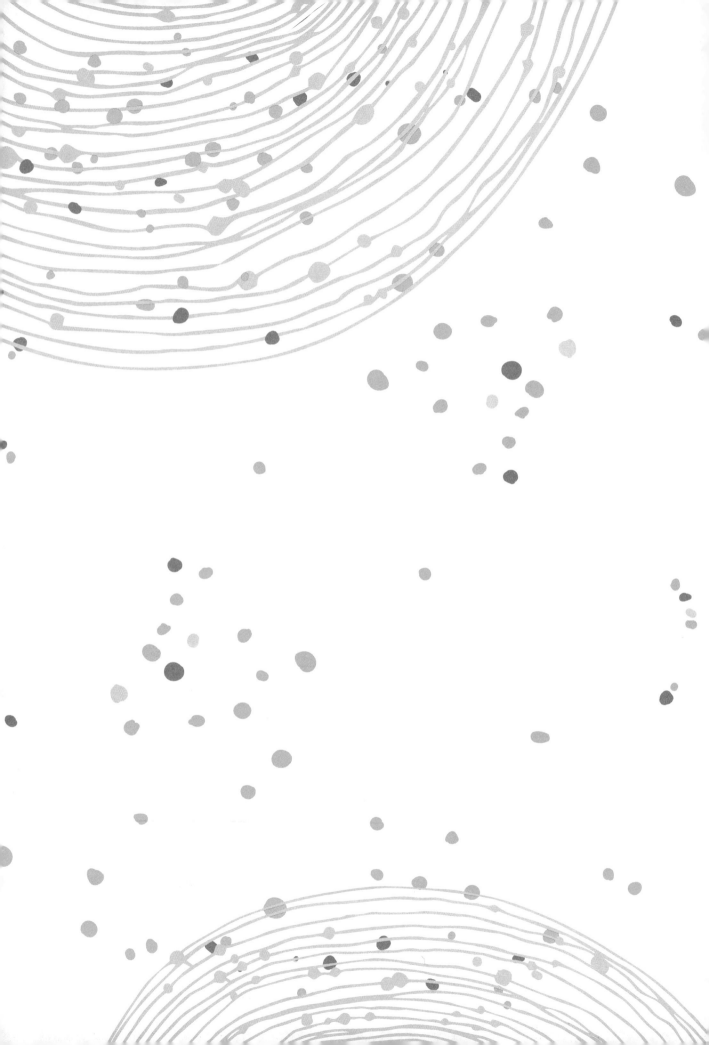

Narrative Writing: Prewriting (B)

Prewrite for Your Personal Narrative

Complete the graphic organizer to plan your personal narrative.

My meaningful moment: _____

1. Plan your **sequence of events**. In each box, describe what will happen in the beginning, middle, and end of your narrative. The middle of your narrative should include a problem that builds up and is solved.

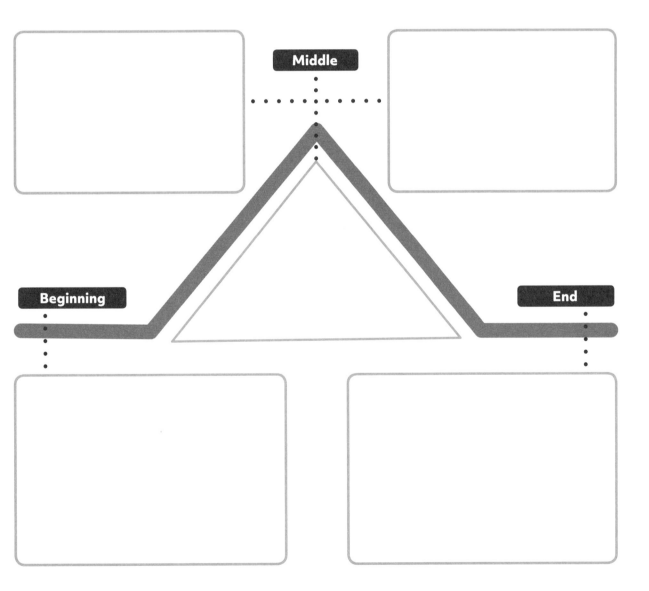

Think about your sequence of events as you answer the questions.

2. What information do readers need to know right away? List important details about the narrator, main characters, setting, and situation.

Narrator	Main Characters	Setting and Situation

3. Think of one important event in your narrative. Write either a short description or a short dialogue that shows readers what happened.

4. Think of one important feeling you had during the events of your narrative. Write description or dialogue that shows readers how you felt.

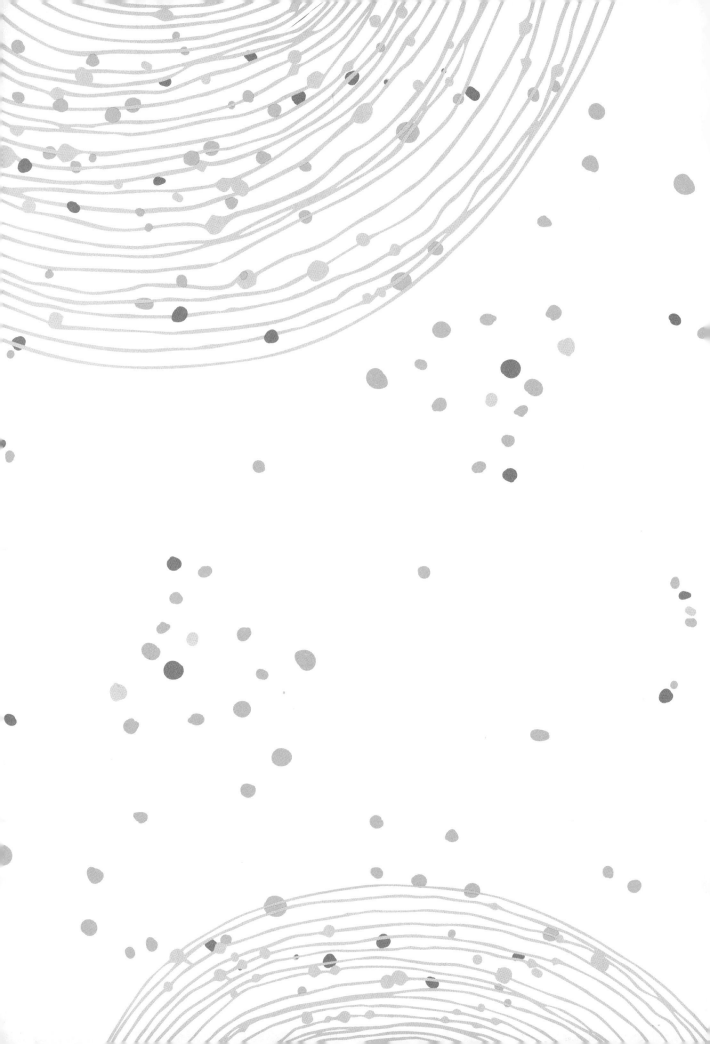

Narrative Writing: Drafting (A)

Draft Your Personal Narrative

Write the first draft of your personal narrative. Write only on the white rows. You will use the purple rows for revisions later.

Title _____

start here ►

keep writing ►

Draft Page 1

keep writing ▶

Draft Page 2

keep writing ▶

Draft Page 3

keep writing ▶

Draft Page 4

keep writing ▶

Draft Page 5

Draft Page 6

Apply: Nuance

Circle the word that best completes the sentence, and explain your choice. Think about the nuances, or small differences in meaning, between the two choices.

1. When his heart beat fast after running, he felt the _____ pulse in his wrist.

   Choices: *prompt*   or   *rapid*

   Explanation:

   _____

   _____

2. The nurse said the need to treat my cut finger was _____ and she would take care of it at once.

   Choices: *rapid*   or   *urgent*

   Explanation:

   _____

   _____

3. You will _____ the way Lana looks in the lovely hat you made for her.

    Choices: *adore*   or   *respect*

    Explanation:

    _____

    _____

4. This award should remind you that we all _____ the way you lead our group.

    Choices: *adore*   or   *respect*

    Explanation:

    _____

    _____

Write your own sentence using one of the given words, but leave a blank space where your chosen word belongs. Have someone else read your sentence. Ask this person to choose which word best belongs in the sentence. Discuss his or her answer.

5. **Choices:** *prompt, rapid,* or *urgent*

    _____

    _____

6. **Choices:** *adore, regard,* or *respect*

    _____

    _____

"Still Standing: The Leaning Tower of Pisa"

Spelling List 5 Pretest

1. **Open the Spelling Pretest activity online. Listen to the first spelling word. Type the word. Check your answer.**

2. **Write the correct spelling of the word in the Word column of the Spelling Pretest table on the next page.**

Word	✓	✗
1 blindfold		

3. **Put a check mark in the ✓ column if you spelled the word correctly online.**

Word	✓	✗
1 blindfold	✓	

   Put an X in the ✗ column if you spelled the word incorrectly online.

Word	✓	✗
1 blindfold		X

4. **Repeat Steps 1–3 for the remaining words in the Spelling Pretest.**

"Still Standing: The Leaning Tower of Pisa"

Spelling List 5 Pretest

Write each spelling word in the Word column, making sure to spell it correctly.

	Word	✓	✗
1			
2			
3			
4			
5			
6			
7			
8			
9			

	Word	✓	✗
10			
11			
12			
13			
14			
15			
16			
17			

"Still Standing: The Leaning Tower of Pisa"

Supporting Author's Points

In a text, authors use reasons or evidence to support an idea or point. Read each question. Answer the questions in complete sentences, using evidence from the text of "Still Standing: The Leaning Tower of Pisa."

1. Answer the questions using information on page 33 of the article.

   a. What happened to the tower as each level was added?

   _____

   _____

   b. What did the builders do to fix the problem?

   _____

   _____

   c. How else does the author describe the builders' actions?

   _____

   _____

2. What point does the author make about the tower on page 34 of the article? Use the questions to guide you.

   a. What happened to the tower when it tilted 5.44 degrees?

   _____

   _____

b. What else does the author say about the tower?

_____

_____

3. In 1992, a scientist and engineers started working on the tower again.
What point does the author make?

_____

_____

_____

_____

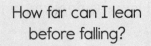

How far can I lean
before falling?

"Still Standing: The Leaning Tower of Pisa" Wrap-Up

Spelling List 5 Activity Bank

Circle any words in the box that you did not spell correctly on the pretest. Using your circled words, complete one activity of your choice. Complete as much of the activity as you can in the time given.

If you spelled all words correctly on the pretest, complete your chosen activity with as many spelling words as you can.

convey	neighborly	weighing	Pennsylvania	substandard
breaking	obey	great	Texas	subtitle
eighty	steakhouse	eighteen	submarine	subway
freighter	survey			

Spelling Activity Choices

Vowel-Free Words

1. In the left column, write only the consonants in each word and put a dot where each vowel should be.

2. Spell each word out loud, stating which vowels should be in the places you wrote dots.

3. In the right column, rewrite the entire spelling word.

4. Correct any spelling errors.

Alphabetizing

1. In the left column, write your words from the spelling word list in alphabetical order.

2. Correct any spelling errors.

Parts of Speech

1. In the left column, write the words from your spelling list that are nouns.

2. In the right column, write all the other words from your spelling list and label each word's part of speech.

3. Correct any spelling errors.

Uppercase and Lowercase

1. In the left column, write each of your words in all capital letters, or all uppercase.

2. In the right column, write each of your words in all lowercase letters.

3. Correct any spelling errors.

Complete the activity that you chose.

My chosen activity: _____

1. _____   _____
2. _____   _____
3. _____   _____
4. _____   _____
5. _____   _____
6. _____   _____
7. _____   _____
8. _____   _____
9. _____   _____
10. _____   _____
11. _____   _____
12. _____   _____
13. _____   _____
14. _____   _____
15. _____   _____
16. _____   _____
17. _____   _____
18. _____   _____
19. _____   _____
20. _____   _____
21. _____   _____
22. _____   _____
23. _____   _____
24. _____   _____
25. _____   _____

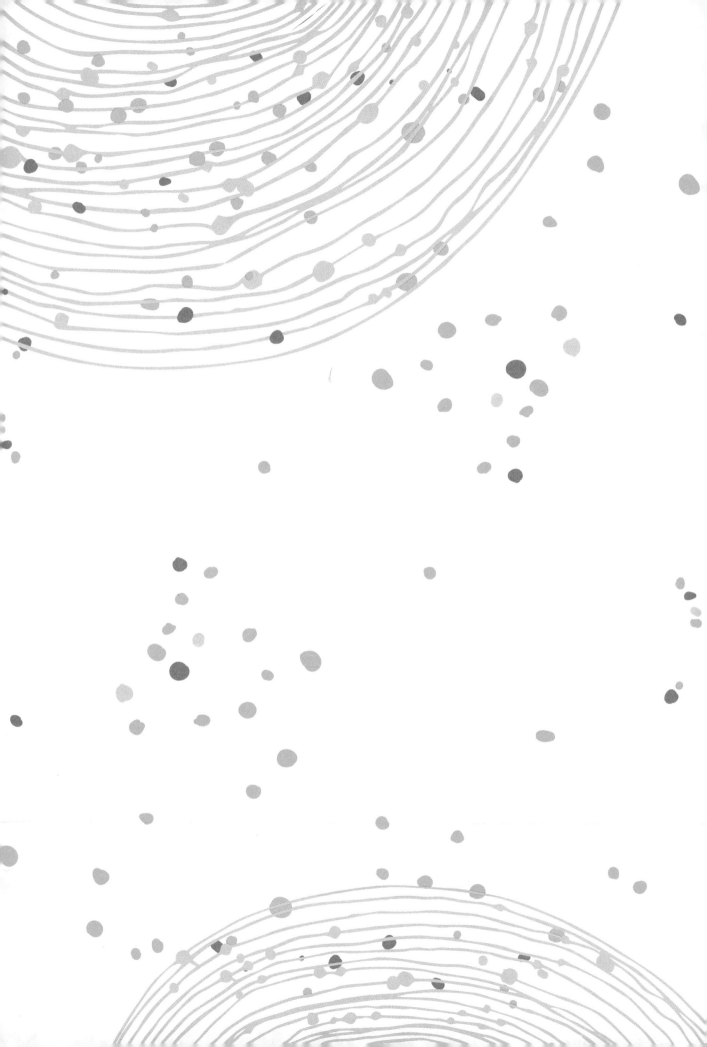

"Still Standing: The Leaning Tower of Pisa" Wrap-Up

Explain the Leaning Tower of Pisa

Use the information on pages 36–37 of the article "Still Standing: The Leaning Tower of Pisa" to explain how the Leaning Tower of Pisa is still standing.

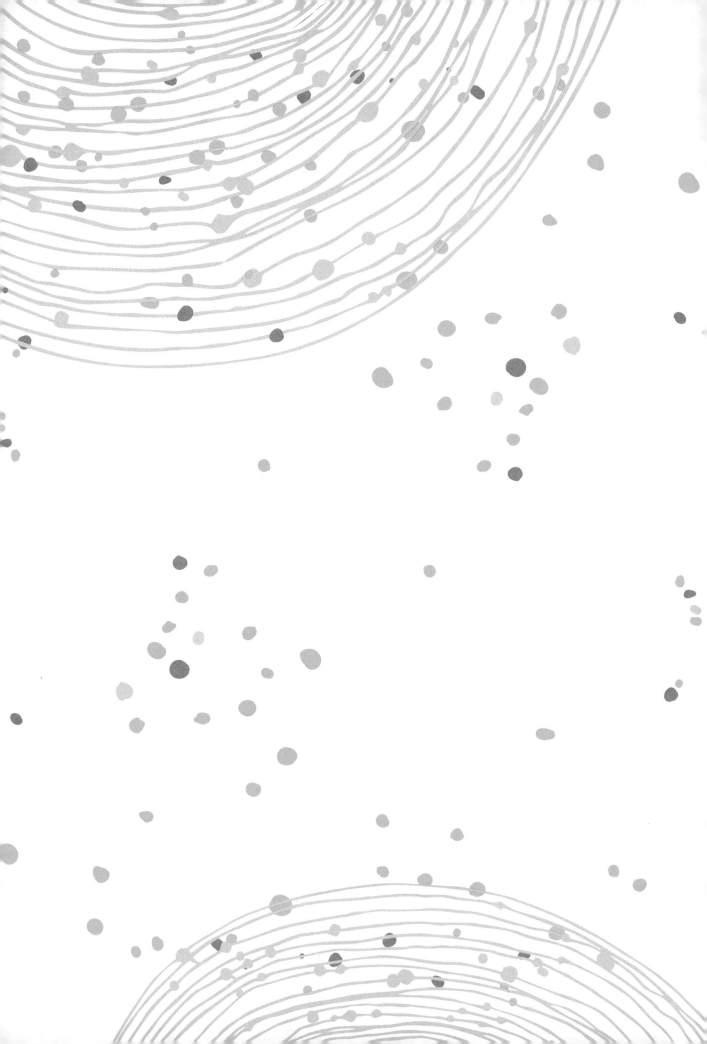

"The Many Colors of Birds"

Write Notes for a Summary

Record notes about the important information on pages 22–23 of "The Many Colors of Birds" in preparation to write a summary. Make sure to include information from the text features, such as the captions and sidebars.

Location	Notes
page 22 Pigmentation	
pages 22–23 Blacks and Browns	
page 23 caption	
page 23 sidebar	

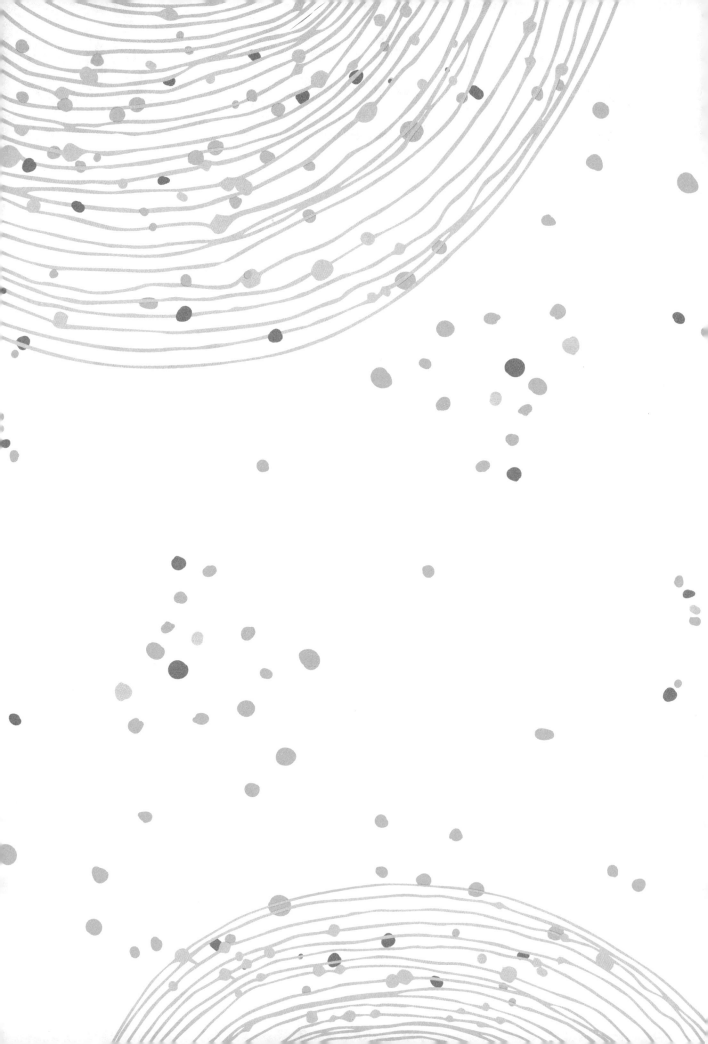

"The Many Colors of Birds" Wrap-Up

Write About Pigmentation

Use the text and your completed Notes for a Summary activity page
from "The Many Colors of Birds." Write a summary that includes all
the important information from the text and the text features.

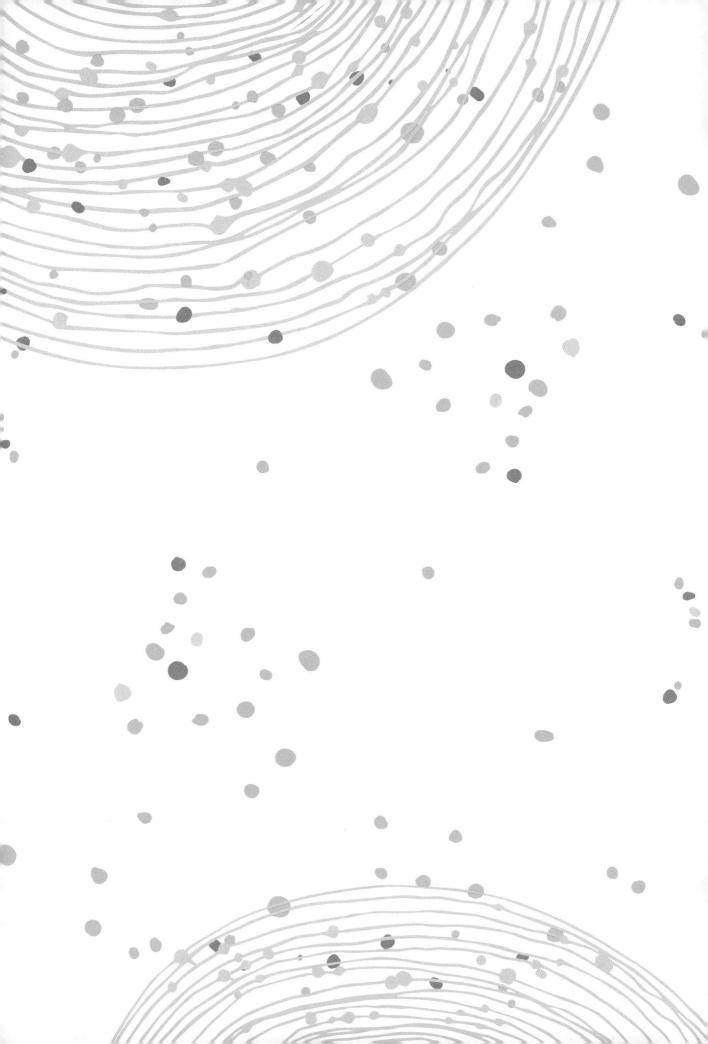

Narrative Writing: Revising

Revise Your Personal Narrative

Use the checklist as you revise your personal narrative draft.

Organization

☐ Does my introduction give enough information about the situation, narrator, and main characters?

☐ Are any ideas in the wrong place?

☐ Do I use clear and logical transitions?

☐ Does my conclusion make sense and answer important questions?

Content

☐ Do I show how the narrator and characters respond to situations by using dialogue or description?

☐ Do I show events by using dialogue or description?

☐ Are there details I can show instead of tell?

☐ Are there words or phrases that could be more concrete?

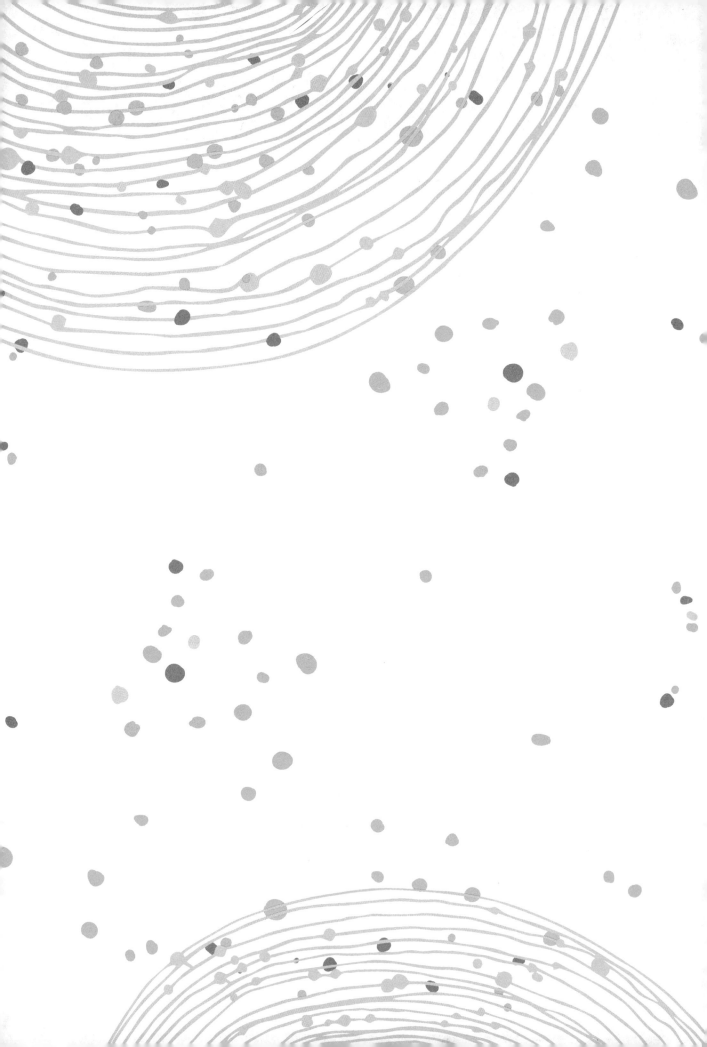

Narrative Writing: Proofreading

Proofread Your Personal Narrative

Use the checklist as you proofread your personal narrative draft.

Grammar and Usage

☐ Are all sentences complete and correct?

☐ Are there any missing or extra words?

☐ Are all verbs in the appropriate tense?

☐ Are adjectives ordered correctly in each sentence?

☐ Are there other grammatical or usage errors?

Mechanics

☐ Is every word spelled correctly, including frequently confused words?

☐ Does every sentence begin with a capital letter and end with the appropriate punctuation?

☐ Is dialogue punctuated correctly?

☐ Are there other punctuation or capitalization errors?

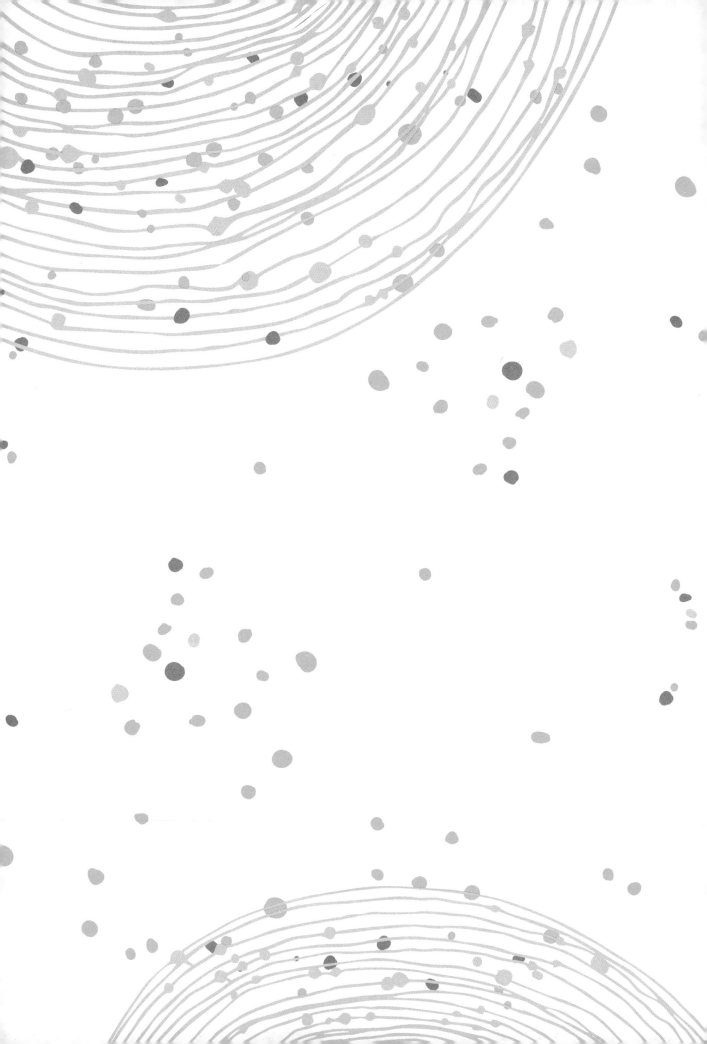

Apply: Precise Words

Circle the word that best completes the sentence, and explain your choice. Think about which choice is the precise word to create the clearest writing.

1. Martin felt nervous as he looked out at the large crowd. He took a deep breath and stepped up to the microphone. He had practiced his speech a million times, but now he couldn't remember a single word. He began to _____ . No matter how hard he tried to speak clearly and smoothly, he couldn't say a complete sentence without stopping and starting.

   Choices: *stammer* or *whisper*

   _____

   _____

   _____

2. The bird flew up to _____ on a small branch near the top of the tree. It seemed to balance easily, even as the wind blew the leaves and branches back and forth. The bird never wobbled or became unsteady as the tree swayed in the breeze.

   Choices: *perch* or *squawk*

   _____

   _____

   _____

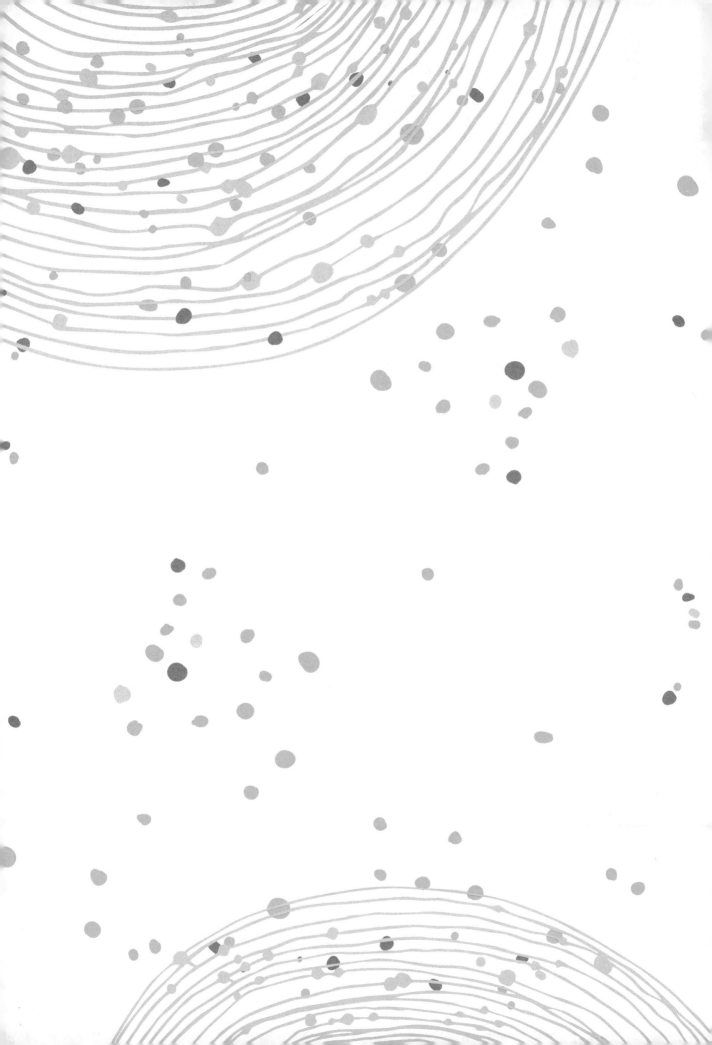

On the Case (A)

Spelling List 6 Pretest

1. Open the Spelling Pretest activity online. Listen to the first spelling word. Type the word. Check your answer.

2. Write the correct spelling of the word in the Word column of the Spelling Pretest table on the next page.

Word	✓	✗
1 blindfold		

3. Put a check mark in the ✓ column if you spelled the word correctly online.

Word	✓	✗
1 blindfold	✓	

Put an X in the ✗ column if you spelled the word incorrectly online.

Word	✓	✗
1 blindfold		✗

4. Repeat Steps 1–3 for the remaining words in the Spelling Pretest.

On the Case (A)

Spelling List 6 Pretest

Write each spelling word in the Word column, making sure to spell it correctly.

	Word	✓	✗
1			
2			
3			
4			
5			
6			
7			
8			
9			

	Word	✓	✗
10			
11			
12			
13			
14			
15			
16			
17			

On the Case (A)

What Do You Know About Juan?

Write your response in complete sentences.

In "The Mystery of the Missing Hamburger," Juan is the story's first-person narrator. He shares his thoughts and feelings with the reader as he tells the story from his point of view. This allows the reader to learn more about Juan and better understand him. Based on the story, what have you learned about Juan? Write a description of him that discusses at least two qualities. Be sure to include details from the passage to support your points.

_____

_____

_____

_____

_____

_____

_____

_____

_____

_____

_____

_____

_____

_____

_____

On the Case (B)

Spelling List 6 Activity Bank

Circle any words in the box that you did not spell correctly on the pretest. Using your circled words, complete one activity of your choice. Complete as much of the activity as you can in the time given.

If you spelled all words correctly on the pretest, complete your chosen activity with as many spelling words as you can.

breathe	evening	remain	obstruction	Tennessee
chimpanzee	extreme	construction	structure	answer
determine	speed	instruct	Alabama	listen
eager	plead			

Spelling Activity Choices

Silly Sentences

1. Write a silly sentence using your words from the spelling word list.

2. Underline the spelling word in each sentence.
   Example: The dog was <u>driving</u> a car.

3. Correct any spelling errors.

Spelling Story

1. Write a very short story using your words from the spelling word list.

2. Underline the spelling words in the story.

3. Correct any spelling errors.

Riddle Me This

1. Write a riddle for your words from the spelling word list.
   Example: "I have a trunk, but it's not on my car."

2. Write the answer, which is your word, for each riddle.
   Example: Answer: elephant

3. Correct any spelling errors.

RunOnWord

1. Gather some crayons, colored pencils, or markers. Write each of your words, using a different color for each word, end to end as one long word.
   Example: dogcatbirdfishturtle

2. Rewrite the words correctly and with proper spacing.

Complete the activity that you chose.

My chosen activity: _____

_____

_____

_____

_____

_____

_____

_____

_____

_____

_____

_____

_____

_____

_____

_____

_____

_____

_____

_____

_____

_____

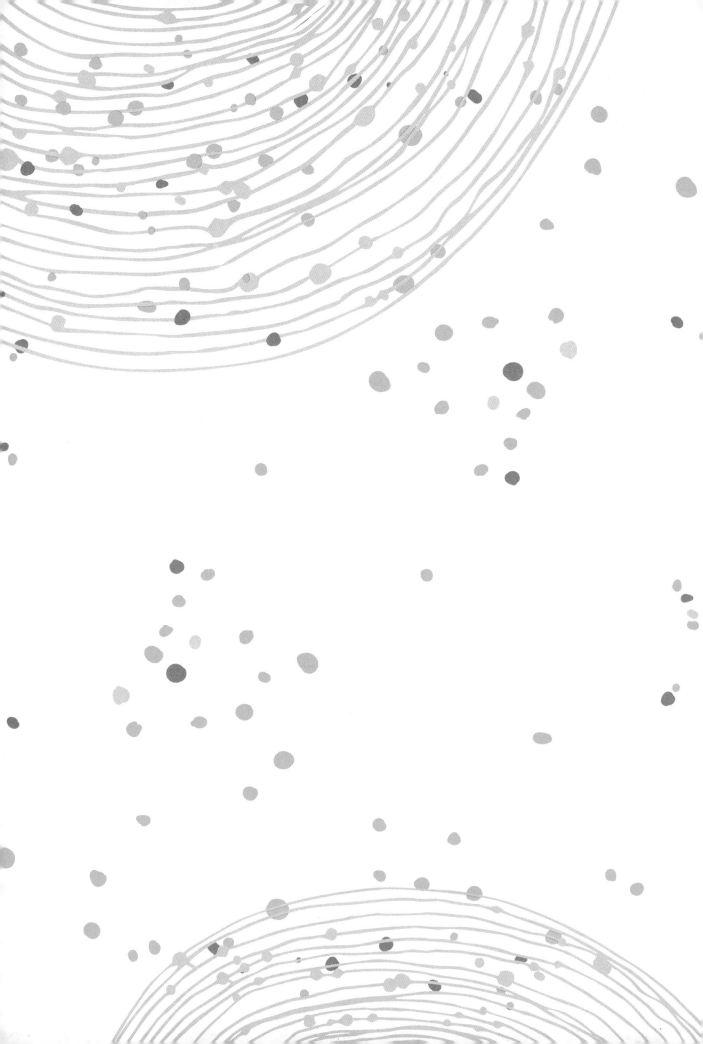

On the Case (B)

Write a Summary of "The Mystery of the Topaz Heart"

Write your response in complete sentences.

Write a one-page summary of "The Mystery of the Topaz Heart." Be sure to include the following:

- Main characters

- Setting

- Most important events from the beginning, middle, and end of the story

Remember that your summary should include only key details.

_____

_____

_____

_____

_____

_____

_____

_____

_____

_____

_____

_____

_____

_____

Writing a summary is a good way to focus on important ideas.

On the Case (C)

Compare the Mysteries

Answer the following questions to compare "The Mystery of the Missing Hamburger" and "The Mystery of the Topaz Heart." Be sure to include details from both stories to support your points.

Title	Setting: Where and when does each story take place, and how are these stories' settings the same and different?
"The Mystery of the Missing Hamburger"	
"The Mystery of the Topaz Heart"	
Both	

Title	Characters: Who are the main characters in each story, and how are they alike and different?
"The Mystery of the Missing Hamburger"	
"The Mystery of the Topaz Heart"	
Both	

Title	Events: How are the events of the two stories alike, and how are they different?
"The Mystery of the Missing Hamburger"	
"The Mystery of the Topaz Heart"	
Both	

Title	Theme: In both stories, one of the big ideas is that paying attention to small details can lead to big discoveries. What details from the texts support this theme?
"The Mystery of the Missing Hamburger"	
"The Mystery of the Topaz Heart"	

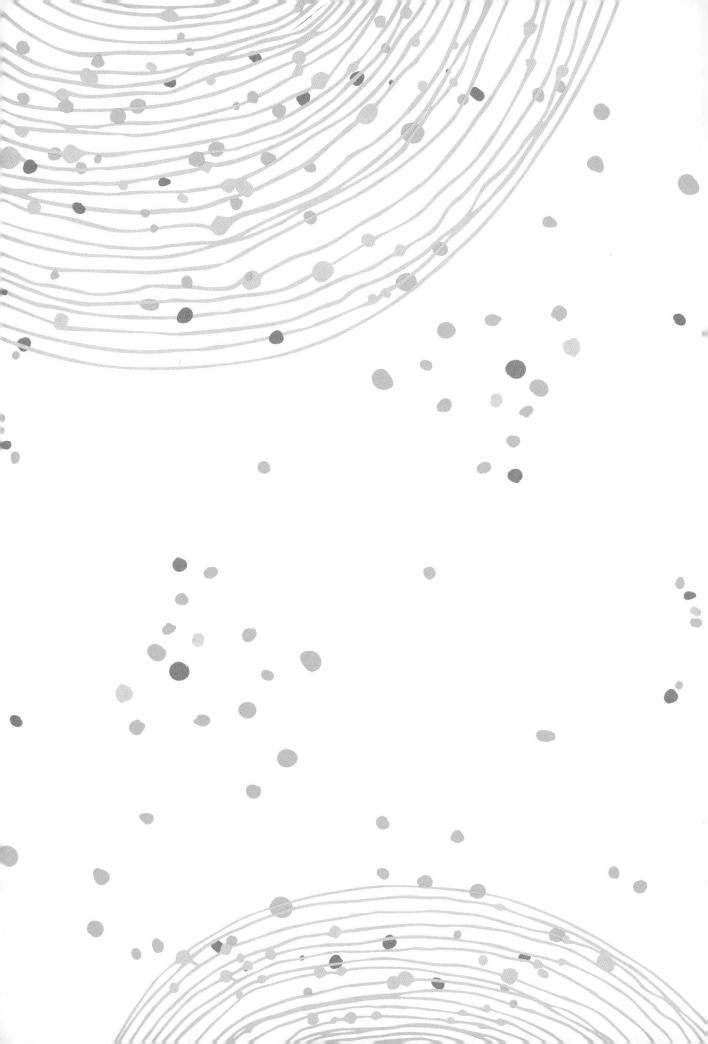

On the Case Wrap-Up

Change the Point of View

Read the passage.

from "The Mystery of the Missing Hamburger"

It was seven on Saturday morning. I was asleep because, well, it was seven on Saturday morning. The phone rang, and I wanted to ignore it, but something told me not to. That something was Mom, who always wakes up before dawn. She was in the den, exercising to a fitness show on TV.

"Answer that, Juan! I'm just getting a good sweat going!" she said.

1. What is the narrator's point of view?

_____

_____

2. List three details about how the narrator tells the story.

_____

_____

_____

from "The Mystery of the Topaz Heart"

Paula took some notes. Then she thanked Bell and Foster for speaking with her and stood to leave. Bell said it was a shame that the topaz heart wouldn't be there to attract visitors to Edgerton anymore. Paula agreed.

"I visited this gallery a lot when I was young," she said. "I loved how the light bounced off the topaz. It was beautiful. It's too bad my daughter may not get to see it herself."

3. What is the narrator's point of view?

_____

4. List three details about how the narrator tells the story.

_____

_____

_____

Write your response in complete sentences.

5. Choose one passage on this activity page to rewrite with a different narrative point of view. If you choose the passage with a first-person narrator, rewrite the passage with a third-person narrator. If you choose the passage with a third-person narrator, rewrite the passage with a first-person narrator. Be sure to include all the details from the original passage in your new passage.

_____

_____

_____

_____

_____

_____

_____

_____

_____

_____

_____

_____

_____

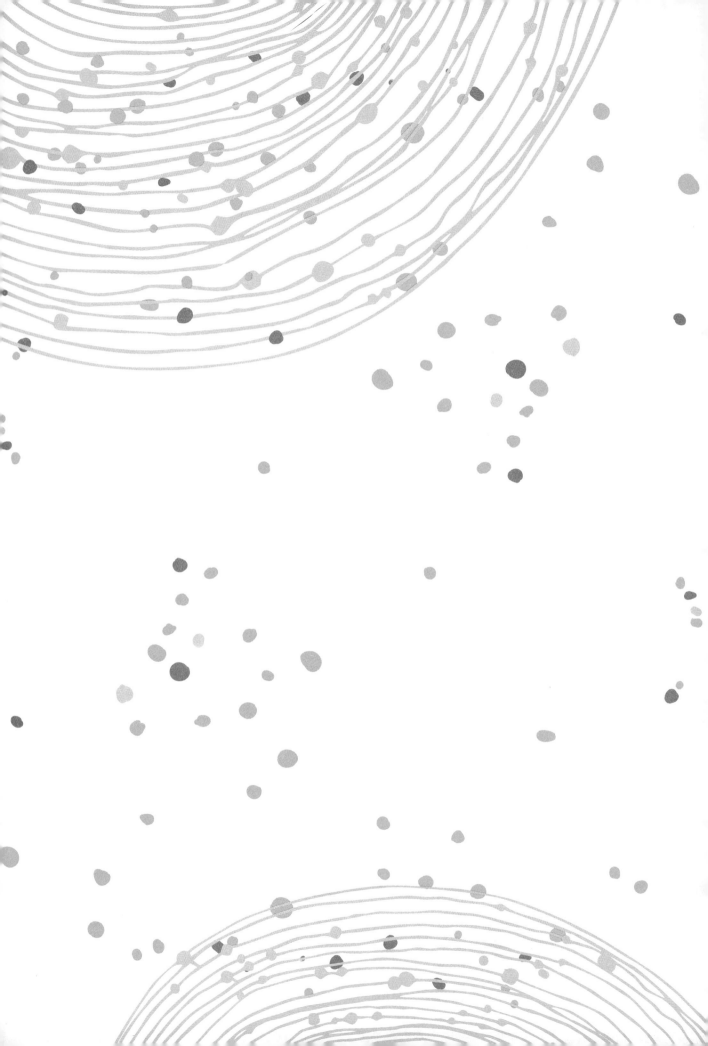

Space Flight (A)

Spelling List 7 Pretest

1. Open the Spelling Pretest activity online. Listen to the first spelling word. Type the word. Check your answer.

2. Write the correct spelling of the word in the Word column of the Spelling Pretest table on the next page.

	Word	✓	✗
1	blindfold		

3. Put a check mark in the ✓ column if you spelled the word correctly online.

	Word	✓	✗
1	blindfold	✓	

Put an X in the ✗ column if you spelled the word incorrectly online.

	Word	✓	✗
1	blindfold		X

4. Repeat Steps 1–3 for the remaining words in the Spelling Pretest.

Space Flight (A)

Spelling List 7 Pretest

Write each spelling word in the Word column, making sure to spell it correctly.

	Word	✓	✕
1			
2			
3			
4			
5			
6			
7			
8			
9			

	Word	✓	✕
10			
11			
12			
13			
14			
15			
16			
17			

Space Flight (A)

Write About the Main Idea

Read the passage. Then answer the questions in complete sentences.

Now the *Friendship 7* capsule was speeding smoothly in orbit. "Capsule is turning around," Glenn reported. And then, "Oh, that view is tremendous!"

Below rolled the wide, blue Earth. Rivers and continents spread out like pages in an atlas. Lightning flickered through storms on the Atlantic. Moonlight silvered the clouds over Africa. On darkened Australia, city lights glowed brightly, turned on as a beacon for the astronaut far overhead.

Over the Pacific, water droplets from the capsule froze into ice particles. They caught the sunlight and floated around *Friendship 7*, looking like fireflies dancing in space.

What is the main idea of this passage? What supporting details led you to this main idea?

_____

_____

_____

_____

_____

Space Flight (B)

Spelling List 7 Activity Bank

Circle any words in the box that you did not spell correctly on the pretest. Using your circled words, complete one activity of your choice. Complete as much of the activity as you can in the time given.

If you spelled all words correctly on the pretest, complete your chosen activity with as many spelling words as you can.

achieve	thief	fantasy	prescribe	New Jersey
believe	agency	greedy	scribble	calendar
ceiling	attorney	scribe	Kentucky	grammar
receive	chimney			

Spelling Activity Choices

Hidden Words

1. Draw a picture and "hide" as many words from the Spelling Word List as they can inside the picture.

2. See if others can find the words within the picture.

Triangle Spelling

Write each word in a triangle.

Ghost Words

1. Use a white crayon to write each spelling word.

2. Go over the white crayon writing with a colored marker.

Complete the activity that you chose.

My chosen activity: _____

Space Flight (B)

Prepare to Write a Firsthand Account

Write your responses in complete sentences.

1. What is a special place you have visited or a special event you have attended?

2. Why did you go to this special place or attend this special event?

3. How would you describe this special place or special event?

4. What are some things you did at this special place or special event? Which of these things was your favorite?

5. What are some of your thoughts, feelings, or opinions about this special place or special event?

_____

_____

_____

A special place doesn't have to be fancy or faraway.

Space Flight (C)

Research for a Secondhand Account

Imagine that you are a reporter. Choose a person to interview, and gather information to answer the following questions. Write your answers in the form of a secondhand account and in complete sentences. For example, *Last summer Anna Lopez visited Yellowstone Park.*

1. What is the name of the person you interviewed?

   _____

2. What is a special place this person has been to or a special event this person has attended?

   _____

   _____

3. Why did this person go to this special place or attend this special event.

   _____

   _____

4. How would this person describe this special place or event?

   _____

   _____

   _____

5. What are some things this person did at this special place or event?

_____

_____

_____

6. What are some facts that this person knows about this special place or event?

_____

_____

_____

_____

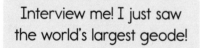

Interview me! I just saw the world's largest geode!

Space Flight Wrap-Up

Write About Firsthand and Secondhand Accounts

Complete the T-chart to explain the features of firsthand and secondhand accounts. Include 3 or more features on each side of the chart.

Firsthand Account | Secondhand Account

Gather your completed Prepare to Write a Firsthand Account and Research for a Secondhand Account activity pages. Use the information from the activity book pages to answer the following questions. Write your responses in complete sentences.

1. Write 2 or 3 sentences that would begin your firsthand account about a special place you have visited or a special event you have attended.

    _____

    _____

    _____

    _____

    _____

    _____

2. Write 2 or 3 sentences that would begin a secondhand account about the person you interviewed for Research for a Secondhand account.

    _____

    _____

    _____

    _____

    _____

    _____

TRY IT

Air and Space Words

Apply: Air and Space Words

Rewrite each sentence or add a second sentence to give a context clue for the meaning of the vocabulary word. Vocabulary words are shown in bold. The first one has been done for you.

1. The pilot sat in the **cockpit** before takeoff.

    New sentence: The pilot sat in the cockpit before takeoff so he could check the controls for operating the plane.

2. My mom worked for many years in **aviation**.

    _____

    _____

3. The captain looked at his **radar**.

    _____

    _____

4. The rocket was **launched** from Kennedy Space Center.

    _____

    _____

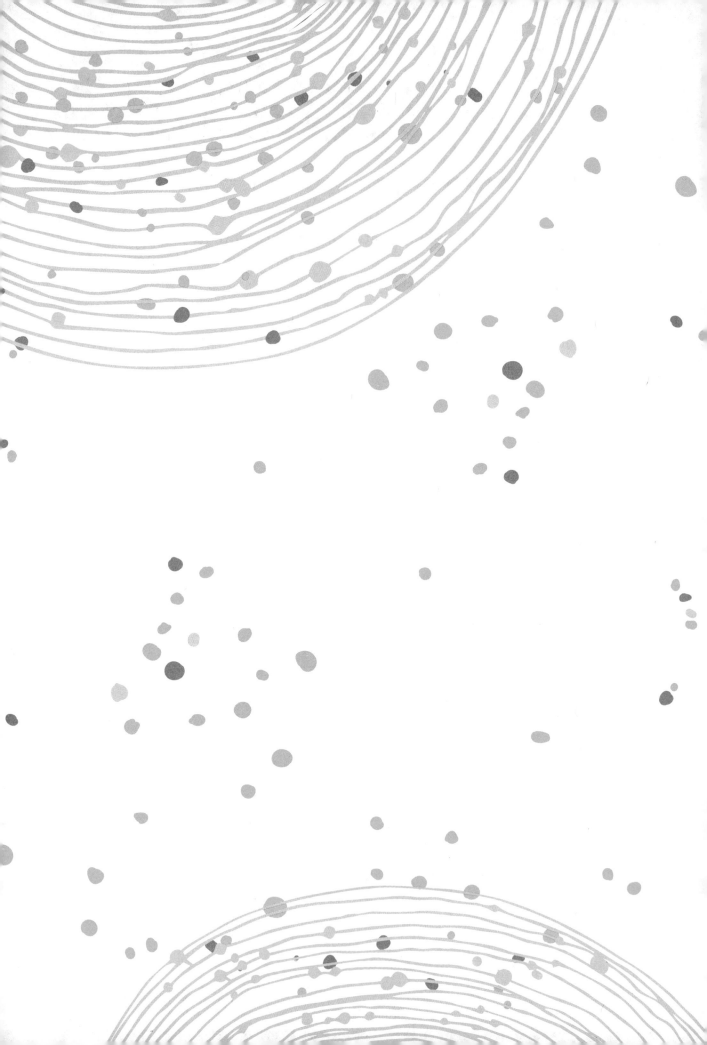

First Flights (A)

Spelling List 8 Pretest

1. Open the Spelling Pretest activity online. Listen to the first spelling word. Type the word. Check your answer.

2. Write the correct spelling of the word in the Word column of the Spelling Pretest table on the next page.

Word	✓	✗
1 blindfold		

3. Put a check mark in the ✓ column if you spelled the word correctly online.

Word	✓	✗
1 blindfold	✓	

   Put an X in the ✗ column if you spelled the word incorrectly online.

Word	✓	✗
1 blindfold		X

4. Repeat Steps 1–3 for the remaining words in the Spelling Pretest.

First Flights (A)

Spelling List 8 Pretest

Write each spelling word in the Word column, making sure to spell it correctly.

	Word	✓	✗
1			
2			
3			
4			
5			
6			
7			
8			
9			

	Word	✓	✗
10			
11			
12			
13			
14			
15			
16			
17			

First Flights (A)

Write About "Wilbur and Orville Wright: Men with Wings"

Read the passage from "Wilbur and Orville Wright: Men with Wings" by Dorothy Haas.

"Which of the Wright brothers," people sometimes ask, "was more responsible for inventing the airplane?"

The brothers would have laughed at such a question. For the answer is: one was as responsible as the other! They thought as a team; when one had an idea, the other was sure to improve on it. And they worked as a team; when they flew their gliders and, finally, their plane, each took a turn at the controls while the other acted as assistant.

The airplane is the amazing result of true teamwork.

Answer the questions in complete sentences.

1. Which sentence from the passage states the main idea of the passage and the story "Wilbur and Orville Wright: Men with Wings"?

_____

_____

_____

2. Write a summary of "Wilbur and Orville Wright: Men with Wings."
Be sure to include details that support the main idea of the story.

_____

_____

_____

_____

_____

_____

_____

_____

_____

_____

_____

_____

_____

_____

_____

_____

_____

_____

_____

_____

_____

_____

_____

_____

First Flights (B)

Spelling List 8 Activity Bank

Circle any words in the box that you did not spell correctly on the pretest. Using your circled words, complete one activity of your choice. Complete as much of the activity as you can in the time given.

If you spelled all words correctly on the pretest, complete your chosen activity with as many spelling words as you can.

analyze	fright	tiger	Rhode Island	patient
apologize	identify	inspect	South Carolina	misjudge
dynamite	license	spectator	everyone	misspell
enlighten	recognize			

Spelling Activity Choices

Create a Crossword

1. Write a word from your spelling word list in the center of the grid paper.

2. Write another spelling word going across and sharing a letter with the first word. See how many words you can connect.

Example:

			p			
		k	i	s	s	e	s
	d		n			
r	o	c	k	s		
	g					
	s					

Word Search Puzzle

1. Draw a box on the grid paper. The box should be large enough to hold your words from the spelling word list.

2. Fill in the grid paper with words from your spelling list, writing them horizontally, vertically, and diagonally (forwards or backwards if you choose).

3. Fill in the rest of the box with random letters.

4. Ask someone to find and circle your spelling words in the puzzle you made.

Complete the activity that you chose.

My chosen activity: _____

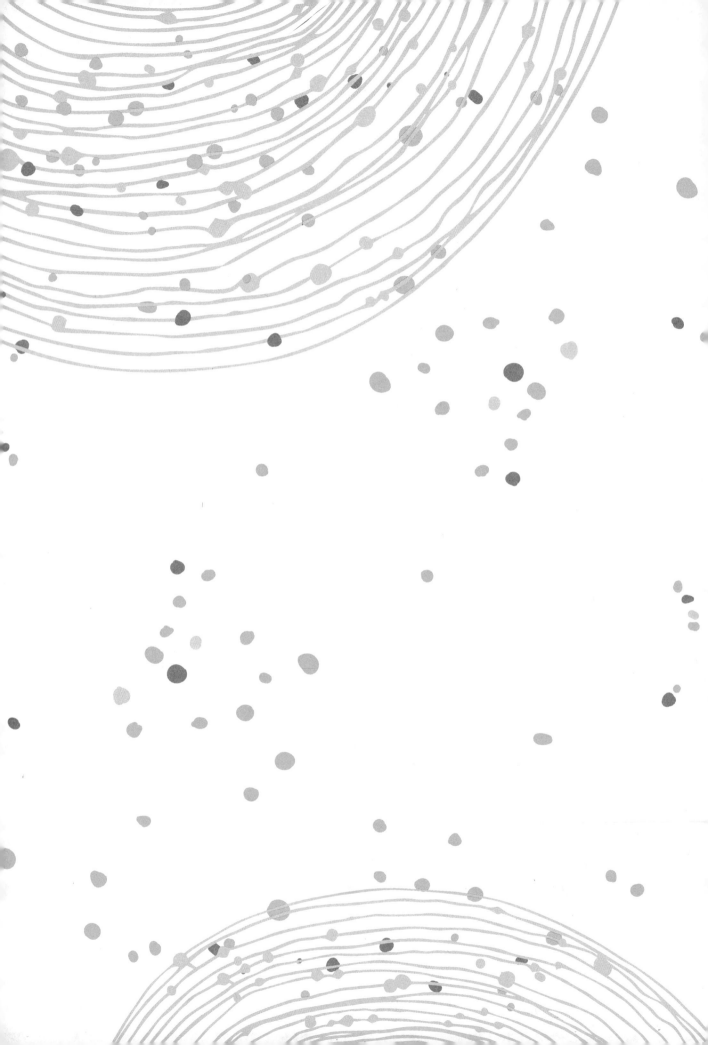

First Flights (B)

Write Notes for Integrating Ideas

Complete the chart with details from each story.

Question	"The Challenge: Bessie Coleman'sStory"	"Dangerous Adventure! Lindbergh's Famous Flight"
Who is the story about?		
What is the main idea of the story?		
When and how did this person become interested in flying?		
What was this person's biggest accomplishment?		

Question	"The Challenge: Bessie Coleman's Story"	"Dangerous Adventure! Lindbergh's Famous Flight"
What challenges did this person face?		
How did this person overcome challenges? Did this person receive help?		
Did this person ever crash? Did it make this person want to quit flying?		
How would you describe this person? (character traits)		

First Flights Wrap-Up

Write About Bessie and Charles

Bessie Coleman and Charles Lindbergh had many things in common. Use your completed Write Notes for Integrating Ideas activity page to help you write about Bessie and Charles.

Answer the questions in complete sentences.

1. What are some things that are similar about Bessie Coleman and Charles Lindbergh?

_____

_____

_____

_____

_____

_____

2. Write at least two paragraphs that combine information from the stories about Bessie Coleman and Charles Lindbergh. Be sure to include what they had in common and specific examples of their individual experiences.

_____

_____

_____

_____

Informational Writing Skills (A)

Spelling List 9 Pretest

1. **Open the Spelling Pretest activity online. Listen to the first spelling word. Type the word. Check your answer.**

2. **Write the correct spelling of the word in the Word column of the Spelling Pretest table on the next page.**

	Word	✓	✕
1	blindfold		

3. **Put a check mark in the ✓ column if you spelled the word correctly online.**

	Word	✓	✕
1	blindfold	✓	

   Put an X in the ✕ column if you spelled the word incorrectly online.

	Word	✓	✕
1	blindfold		X

4. **Repeat Steps 1–3 for the remaining words in the Spelling Pretest.**

Informational Writing Skills (A)

Spelling List 9 Pretest

Write each spelling word in the Word column, making sure to spell it correctly.

	Word	✓	✗
1			
2			
3			
4			
5			
6			
7			
8			
9			

	Word	✓	✗
10			
11			
12			
13			
14			
15			
16			
17			

Informational Writing Skills (A)

Write an Informational Paragraph

Use the prompt to answer the questions.

Prompt: **Write an informational paragraph about a town or a city.**

1. Which town or city will you write about? Choose a place that you know well.

   _____

2. Strong informational writing begins with a **hook** that grabs the attention and interest of readers. Write a hook to begin your paragraph.

   _____

   _____

   _____

3. A **topic sentence** expresses the main idea of a paragraph. Write a topic sentence for your paragraph.

   _____

   _____

   _____

4. What information will you include to support your topic sentence? Describe at least three supporting ideas in the order that you'll write them. You do not need to research these ideas at this time.

   a. _____

   _____

   _____

   b. _____

   _____

   _____

   c. _____

   _____

5. Images can help readers understand your informational paragraph.

   a. Describe, sketch, or paste a copy of an image that would help readers understand your paragraph.

   _____

   b. Explain how your image will help readers understand your paragraph.

   _____

   _____

Informational Writing Skills (B)

Spelling List 9 Activity Bank

Circle any words in the box that you did not spell correctly on the pretest. Using your circled words, complete one activity of your choice. Complete as much of the activity as you can in the time given.

If you spelled all words correctly on the pretest, complete your chosen activity with as many spelling words as you can.

approach	foe	thrown	valuable	inadequate
boastful	growth	tomorrow	Nevada	incomplete
bowling	oboe	evaluate	New York	incorrect
coastal	throat			

Spelling Activity Choices

Vowel-Free Words

1. In the left column, write only the consonants in each word and put a dot where each vowel should be.

2. Spell each word out loud, stating which vowels should be in the places you wrote dots.

3. In the right column, rewrite the entire spelling word.

4. Correct any spelling errors.

Alphabetizing

1. In the left column, write your words from the spelling word list in alphabetical order.

2. Correct any spelling errors.

Parts of Speech

1. In the left column, write the words from your spelling list that are nouns.

2. In the right column, write all the other words from your spelling list and label each word's part of speech.

3. Correct any spelling errors.

Uppercase and Lowercase

1. In the left column, write each of your words in all capital (uppercase) letters.

2. In the right column, write each of your words in all lowercase letters.

3. Correct any spelling errors.

Complete the activity that you chose.

My chosen activity: _____

1. _____ _____
2. _____ _____
3. _____ _____
4. _____ _____
5. _____ _____
6. _____ _____
7. _____ _____
8. _____ _____
9. _____ _____
10. _____ _____
11. _____ _____
12. _____ _____
13. _____ _____
14. _____ _____
15. _____ _____
16. _____ _____
17. _____ _____
18. _____ _____
19. _____ _____
20. _____ _____
21. _____ _____
22. _____ _____
23. _____ _____
24. _____ _____
25. _____ _____

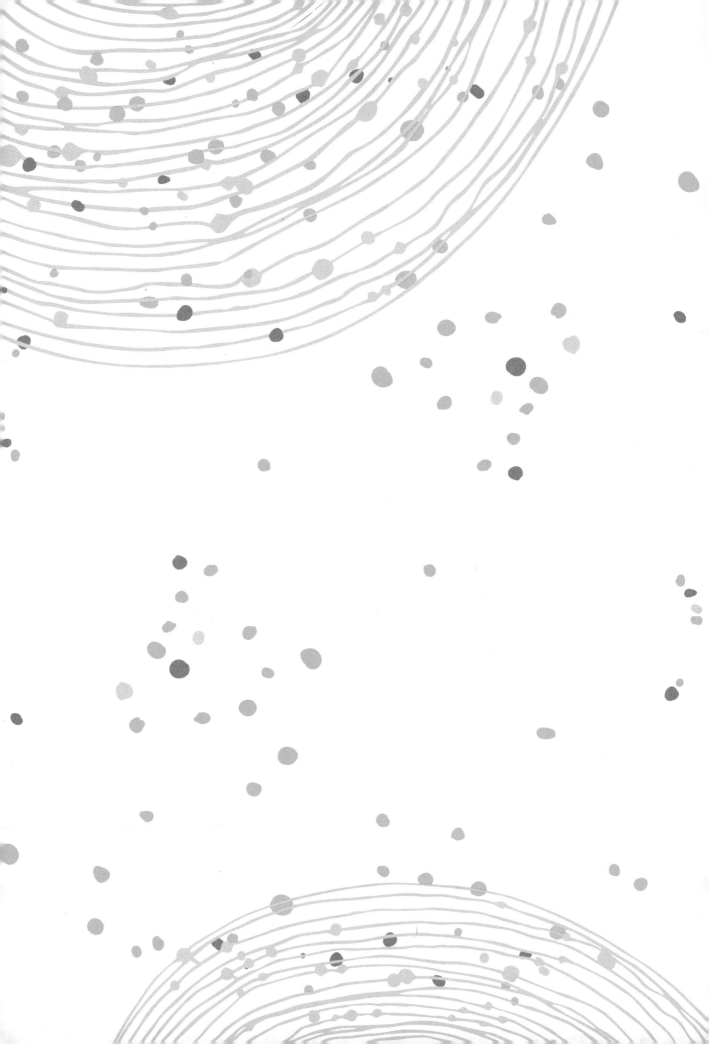

Informational Writing Skills (B)

Develop Your Topic

Use the prompt to answer the questions.

Prompt: **Write an informational paragraph about a town or a city.**

Write your informational paragraph.

- Write a title.

- Write your hook and topic sentence.

- Write your supporting ideas. Use facts, concrete details, quotations, definitions, and examples to develop your ideas. If needed, research your ideas using a reliable website or other reference. You can even conduct an interview.

- Use at least one transition in your paragraph to connect your ideas. Underline the transitions you use.

Informational Writing Skills (C)

Finish Your Informational Paragraph

Use the prompt to answer the questions.

Prompt: **Write an informational paragraph about a town or a city.**

1. Revise at least one sentence from your paragraph to use domain-specific language. For instance, you might use the terms *founded*, *population*, or *city limits*.

    a. Original sentence:

    _____

    _____

    b. Revised sentence:

    _____

    _____

2. Revise at least one sentence from your paragraph to use more precise language. For example, you might refer to a specific location or event.

    a. Original sentence:

    _____

    _____

    b. Revised sentence:

    _____

    _____

3. Revise at least one sentence from your paragraph to be more formal. For example, you might revise slang, incorrect grammar, or abbreviations.

    a. Original sentence:

        _____

        _____

    b. Revised sentence:

        _____

        _____

4. Write a concluding sentence for your paragraph. The conclusion should wrap up the text and stress its overall meaning or importance.

    _____

    _____

    _____

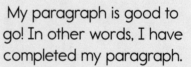

My paragraph is good to go! In other words, I have completed my paragraph.

Informational Writing Skills Wrap-Up

Use Informational Writing Skills

Use the prompt and the facts to answer the questions.

Prompt: **Write an informational paragraph about Amelia Earhart.**

Facts:

- Born in Kansas in 1897

- First saw a plane when she was 10

- **1920:** First flew on a plane; took her first flying lesson less than a week later

- **1923:** Earned her pilot's license

- **1928:** Served as navigator on a flight across the Atlantic Ocean

- **1929:** Worked to organize the Ninety-Nines, a group of female pilots who urged more women to learn to fly

- **1931:** Set a world record for altitude (height) by flying to over 18,000 feet

- **1932:** Became first woman to complete a solo transatlantic (across the Atlantic Ocean) flight

- **1932:** Became first woman to fly solo across the United States (California to New Jersey)

- **1935:** Became first woman to fly solo from Hawaii to California

- **1937:** Attempted to be the first pilot to fly around the world; disappeared over the Pacific Ocean

1. A hook grabs readers' attention. Write a hook to begin your informational paragraph about Amelia Earhart.

_____

_____

_____

2. The topic sentence states the main idea of the paragraph. Write a topic sentence that states the main idea of your informational paragraph.

_____

_____

_____

3. Using the facts provided, write at least three sentences to support your main idea. You do not need to include every fact.

_____

_____

_____

_____

_____

_____

_____

4. Transitions connect and relate ideas in an informational text.

   a. List at least one transition you included in your answer to Question 3.

   _____

   _____

   _____

   b. Explain how the transition improves reader understanding.

   _____

   _____

   _____

5. An informational paragraph uses precise, formal language.

   a. Rewrite one sentence in your paragraph to make the language more precise.

   _____

   _____

   _____

   b. Rewrite any sentences in your paragraph that do not use formal language.

   _____

   _____

   _____

c. Rewrite at least one sentence in your paragraph to include language that is specific to the field of aviation.

_____

_____

_____

_____

6. Write a short conclusion to your paragraph. Your conclusion should help readers understand why your main idea was important.

_____

_____

7. Informational writing often contains graphics that help readers understand the subject or give them a clear mental picture of people or events described in the passage. Describe one visual aid that might be included in your informational paragraph about Amelia Earhart.

_____

_____

Spelling List 10 Pretest

1. **Open the Spelling Pretest activity online. Listen to the first spelling word. Type the word. Check your answer.**

2. **Write the correct spelling of the word in the Word column of the Spelling Pretest table on the next page.**

Word	✓	✗
1 blindfold		

3. **Put a check mark in the ✓ column if you spelled the word correctly online.**

Word	✓	✗
1 blindfold	✓	

   Put an X in the ✗ column if you spelled the word incorrectly online.

Word	✓	✗
1 blindfold		✗

4. **Repeat Steps 1–3 for the remaining words in the Spelling Pretest.**

Pax (A)

Spelling List 10 Pretest

Write each spelling word in the Word column, making sure to spell it correctly.

	Word	✓	✗
1			
2			
3			
4			
5			
6			
7			
8			
9			
10			
11			

	Word	✓	✗
12			
13			
14			
15			
16			
17			
18			
19			
20			
21			

Pax (A)

Describe Peter and Pax

Choose the character traits that describe Peter and Pax. Then write a paragraph about each character. Use complete sentences in your paragraphs.

1. Circle the traits that describe Peter.

   has anxiety   tall   scared

   angry   strong-willed   connected to Pax

2. Choose one of Peter's traits that you circled. Write a paragraph that explains how you know that Peter has that trait. Be sure to include a detail from the story that shows how you know.

   _____

   _____

   _____

   _____

   _____

   _____

3. Circle the traits that describe Pax.

   loyal   brave   strong sense of touch

   trusting   loving   strong sense of smell

4. Choose one of Pax's traits that you circled. Write a paragraph that explains how you know that Pax has that trait. Be sure to include a detail from the story that shows how you know.

_____

_____

_____

_____

_____

_____

_____

Spelling List 10 Activity Bank

Circle any words in the box that you did not spell correctly on the pretest. Using your circled words, complete one activity of your choice. Complete as much of the activity as you can in the time given.

If you spelled all words correctly on the pretest, complete your chosen activity with as many spelling words as you can.

global	though	decompose	interrupt	biannual
soldier	motivate	diagnose	rupture	bicycle
buffalo	telescope	disrupt	New Mexico	bimonthly
earlobe	trombone	erupt	Oklahoma	biweekly
doughnut				

Spelling Activity Choices

Silly Sentences

1. Write a silly sentence using your words from the spelling word list.

2. Underline the spelling word in each sentence.
   Example: The dog was <u>driving</u> a car.

3. Correct any spelling errors.

Spelling Story

1. Write a very short story using your words from the spelling word list.

2. Underline the spelling words in the story.

3. Correct any spelling errors.

Riddle Me This

1. Write a riddle for your words from the spelling word list.
   Example: "I have a trunk, but it's not on my car."

2. Write the answer, which is your word, for each riddle.
   Example: Answer: elephant

3. Correct any spelling errors.

RunOnWord

1. Gather some crayons, colored pencils, or markers. Write each of your words, using a different color for each word, end to end as one long word.
   Example: dogcatbirdfishturtle

2. Rewrite the words correctly and with proper spacing.

Complete the activity that you chose.

My chosen activity: _____

_____

_____

_____

_____

_____

_____

_____

_____

_____

_____

_____

_____

_____

_____

_____

_____

_____

_____

_____

_____

_____

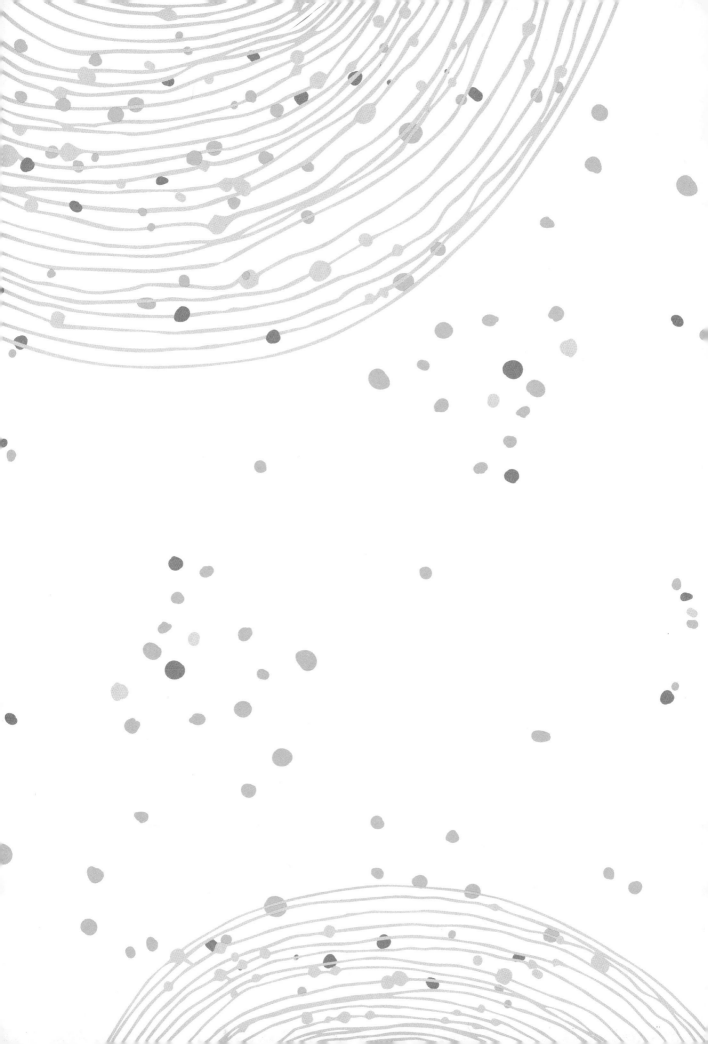

Write About Setting

The author of *Pax* does not give specific details about the setting of the story. Write descriptions that are specific about where and when the story could be happening. Include your own ideas as well as details from the story. Use complete sentences in your answers.

1. Describe the setting around the baseball field where Peter sleeps in the dugout. Does this place have a name? Is it a large city or a small town? Use details from the text and your own ideas to describe this place.

2. Part of any setting is when a story happens. Describe a time when the novel *Pax* could be taking place. What year could it be when the war is coming and Peter must return Pax to the wild? Use details from the story and your imagination to support your ideas.

_____

_____

_____

_____

_____

_____

Write About What's Happened So Far

Use complete sentences in your answers.

1. Who are the main characters so far?

   _____

   _____

2. Where have Peter and Pax been so far? What is the setting?

   _____

   _____

   _____

   _____

   _____

   _____

   _____

3. Summarize what has happened so far. Remember that a summary includes only the most important events and details.

   _____

   _____

   _____

   _____

   _____

   _____

_____

_____

_____

_____

_____

_____

_____

_____

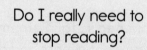

Do I really need to stop reading?

Write About Characters and Plot

You have learned that characters affect a plot's events. Imagine how the events would change if characters did things differently. Use complete sentences in your answers.

1. How do you imagine the plot would change if Peter had not gone to Vola's barn after he broke his foot? Write a paragraph explaining your ideas.

2. How do you imagine the plot would change if Runt had not invited Pax to come with him back to his and Bristle's home? Write a paragraph explaining your ideas.

_____

_____

_____

_____

_____

_____

_____

_____

_____

_____

_____

_____

Change the Setting

Choose a favorite story. Think about how the story would be different if the setting were different. Use complete sentences in your answers.

1. What is the title of your favorite story?

    _____

2. Imagine that your favorite story has a different setting. What would that setting be like?

    _____

    _____

    _____

    _____

    _____

    _____

    _____

    _____

    _____

    _____

3. How would the events of the story's plot change if the setting were different? Describe at least two ways the events would change because of the new setting.

_____

_____

_____

_____

_____

_____

_____

_____

_____

_____

_____

_____

Pax (F)

Spelling List 11 Pretest

1. Open the Spelling Pretest activity online. Listen to the first spelling word. Type the word. Check your answer.

2. Write the correct spelling of the word in the Word column of the Spelling Pretest table on the next page.

Word	✓	✗
1 blindfold		

3. Put a check mark in the ✓ column if you spelled the word correctly online.

Word	✓	✗
1 blindfold	✓	

Put an X in the ✗ column if you spelled the word incorrectly online.

Word	✓	✗
1 blindfold		X

4. Repeat Steps 1–3 for the remaining words in the Spelling Pretest.

Pax (F)

Spelling List 11 Pretest

Write each spelling word in the Word column, making sure to spell it correctly.

	Word	✓	✗
1			
2			
3			
4			
5			
6			
7			
8			
9			
10			
11			

	Word	✓	✗
12			
13			
14			
15			
16			
17			
18			
19			
20			
21			

Pax (F)

Summarize Events

Summarize what has happened in *Pax*, Chapters 10–18.
Use complete sentences in your answers.

1. What has happened to Peter in Chapters 10–18?

_____

_____

_____

_____

_____

_____

_____

_____

_____

_____

_____

_____

_____

_____

_____

_____

_____

2. What has happened to Pax in Chapters 10–18?

_____

_____

_____

_____

_____

_____

_____

_____

_____

_____

_____

_____

_____

_____

_____

Spelling List 11 Activity Bank

Circle any words in the box that you did not spell correctly on the pretest. Using your circled words, complete one activity of your choice. Complete as much of the activity as you can in the time given.

If you spelled all words correctly on the pretest, complete your chosen activity with as many spelling words as you can.

issue	pupil	university	Georgia	semicircle
community	refugee	dictator	Virginia	semifinal
commute	uniform	dictionary	against	semipro
cue	union	predict	restaurant	semiformal
execute				

Spelling Activity Choices

Hidden Words

1. Draw a picture and "hide" as many words from the Spelling Word List as you can inside the picture.

2. See if others can find the words within the picture.

Triangle Spelling

Write each word in a triangle.

Ghost Words

1. Use a white crayon to write each spelling word.

2. Go over the white crayon writing with a colored marker.

Complete the activity that you chose.

My chosen activity: _____

They Live in a Cauldron?

You've learned that a group of foxes is called a *skulk* and a group of crows is called a *murder*. Learn the names of other animal groups, and write a short story about one. Use complete sentences in your story.

1. Draw lines to match the name of the animal grouping to the animal.

These winged mammals sleep in dark places during the day and hunt at night. They live in a group called a **cauldron**.

penguins

These large animals have trunks. They live in a group called a **parade**.

giraffes

These flightless birds use their wings for swimming in the cold ocean at the bottom of the world. They live in a group called a **colony**.

elephants

These animals have very long necks to reach the tops of trees. They live in a group called a **tower**.

kangaroos

These Australian animals have pouches. They live in a group called a **mob**.

bats

2. Choose an animal grouping from Question 1. If you like, you may choose a grouping not in the matching activity, such as "a murder of crows" or "a skulk of foxes." Write a very short story about your chosen animal grouping. Make sure your story has a beginning, middle, and end.

_____

_____

_____

_____

_____

_____

_____

_____

_____

_____

_____

Can I ask a troop of baboons to help me write my story?

How a Picture Makes You Feel

Look at the picture on page 239 of *Pax*. Answer the questions.
Use complete sentences in your answers.

1. What is happening in the picture on page 239?

_____

_____

_____

_____

_____

_____

2. How do you think Peter feels in the picture? How does the picture
   make you feel? Why?

_____

_____

_____

_____

_____

_____

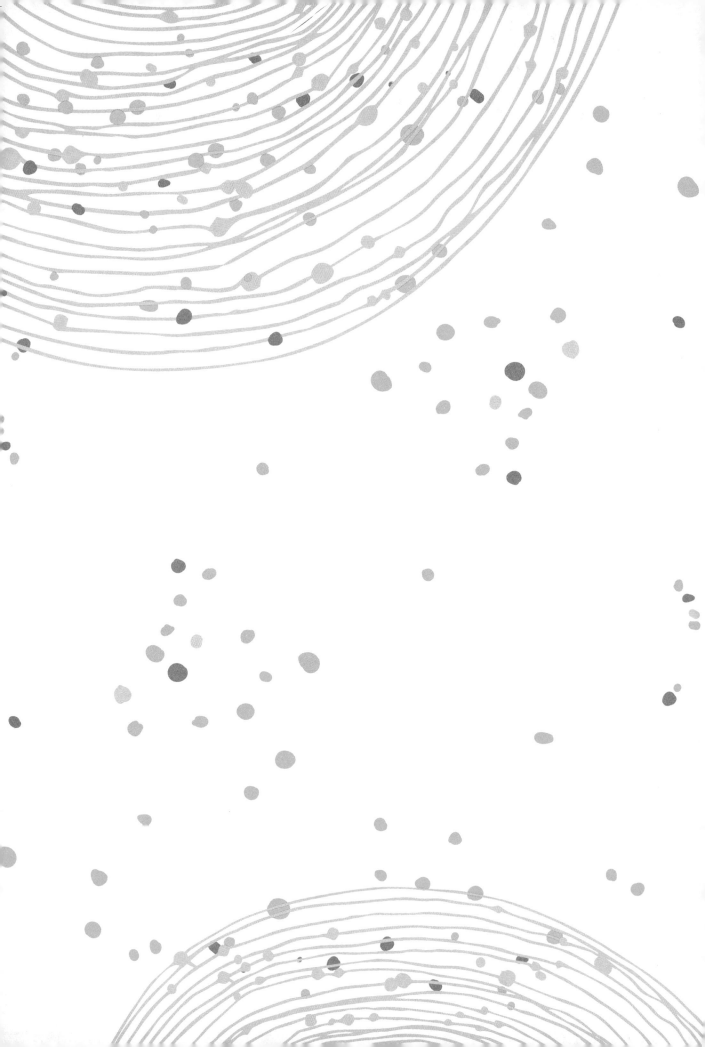

Write About Theme in *Pax*

Answer the questions. Use complete sentences in your answers.

1. What is one of the themes in the novel *Pax*?

    _____

    _____

2. How do details from the story, including characters' actions, support the theme you identified in Question 1?

    _____

    _____

    _____

    _____

    _____

    _____

    _____

    _____

    _____

    _____

    _____

    _____

    _____

    _____

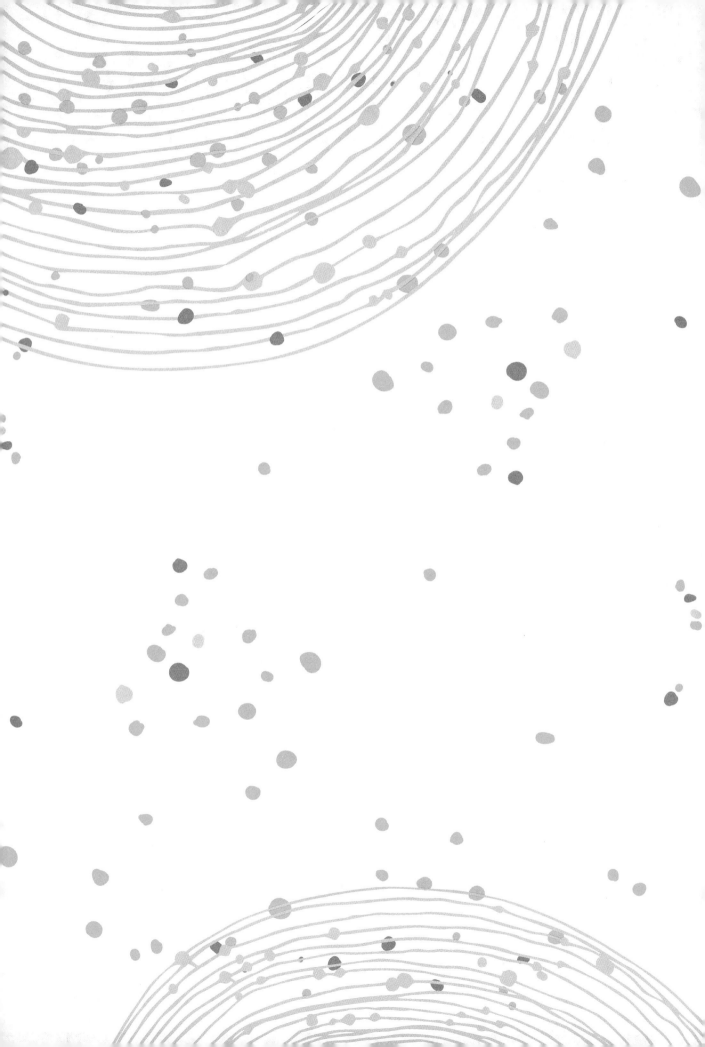

Pax Wrap-Up

Write a Summary of *Pax*

Remember: A good summary includes the most important events, characters, and key details in a story. Events in a summary should be described in the order they happen in the story.

Write a 1- to 2-page summary of *Pax*. Write your response in complete sentences.

Similes

Apply: Similes

Rewrite the following sentences or add a second sentence that makes the meaning of the simile clear. The first one has been done for you.

1. The instructions for my new game are **clear as mud**.

   New sentence:

   The instructions for my new game are clear as mud. They are so confusing that I can't begin to play.

2. My best friend **sleeps like a log**.

   _____

   _____

3. The soccer player **ran like the wind** to score the winning goal.

   _____

   _____

4. My dad has **eyes like a hawk** when it comes to me eating candy.

   _____

   _____

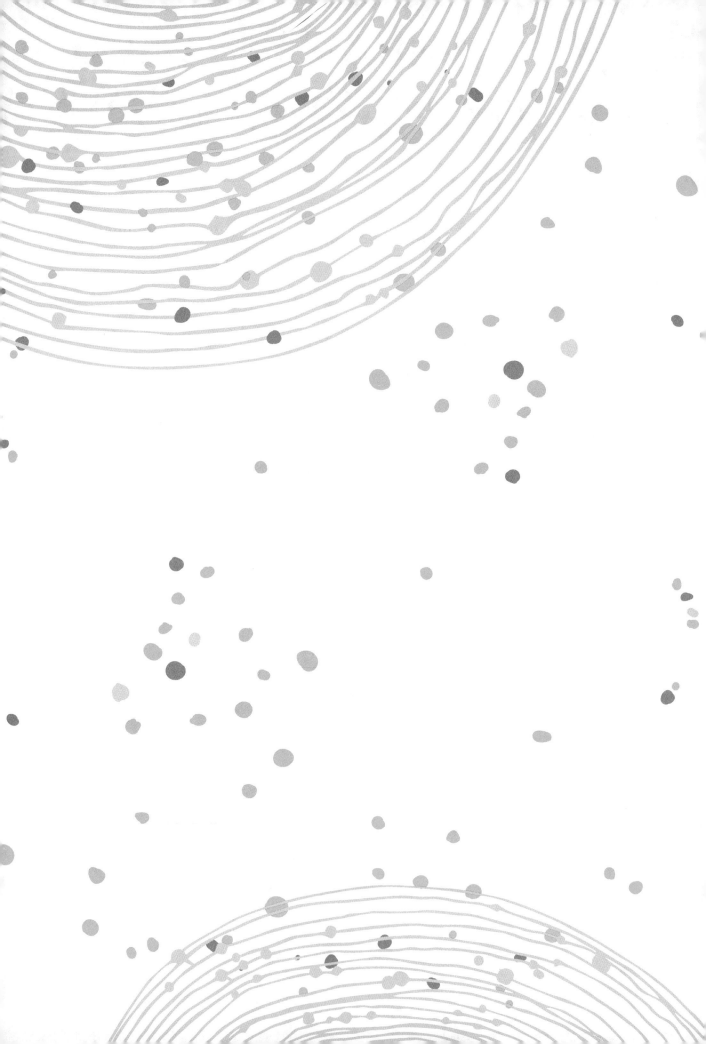

Informational Writing: Prewriting (A)

Spelling List 12 Pretest

1. Open the Spelling Pretest activity online. Listen to the first spelling word. Type the word. Check your answer.

2. Write the correct spelling of the word in the Word column of the Spelling Pretest table on the next page.

Word	✓	✗
1 blindfold		

3. Put a check mark in the ✓ column if you spelled the word correctly online.

Word	✓	✗
1 blindfold	✓	

Put an X in the ✗ column if you spelled the word incorrectly online.

Word	✓	✗
1 blindfold		X

4. Repeat Steps 1–3 for the remaining words in the Spelling Pretest.

Informational Writing: Prewriting (A)

Spelling List 12 Pretest

Write each spelling word in the Word column, making sure to spell it correctly.

	Word	✓	✗
1			
2			
3			
4			
5			
6			
7			
8			
9			
10			
11			

	Word	✓	✗
12			
13			
14			
15			
16			
17			
18			
19			
20			
21			

Informational Writing: Prewriting (A)

Brainstorm for Your History Report

Read the writing assignment. You will complete the assignment in steps over multiple lessons.

Prompt: **Write a report on a history-related topic. Your topic can be a historical event or person.**

Requirements: Your report should include the following:

- A **title**

- An **introduction** that names the topic and includes relevant background information

- **Three body paragraphs** with important facts and details

- A **conclusion** that sums up key points and wraps up the text

- **Headings** that separate different sections of text and briefly describe what the text that follows will address

- Information discovered during research, including at least one **direct quotation**

- At least one **image, illustration, chart**, or **multimedia element**

- **Domain-specific language** and **transitions** to connect and relate ideas

- Correct **grammar, usage**, and **mechanics**

- A list of at least **two trustworthy sources**, one of which is a print source, such as a newspaper, magazine, book, or encyclopedia. The other source may be a digital source found on the Internet, such as a government website.

Audience: Your teacher and peers

Purpose: Inform or explain your topic to readers.

Length: 400 to 600 words long (approximately 6–8 handwritten drafting pages or ($1\frac{1}{2}$ to 2 pages typed and double spaced)

Brainstorm and choose a topic for your history report. As you brainstorm, you may add more circles to the web.

1. In the circles connected to "History Report," name at least three broad history categories that interest you, such as *American Revolution* or *past presidents*.

2. In the circles connected to each broad category, name at least two topics related to that category, such as *George Washington* or *Thomas Jefferson*.

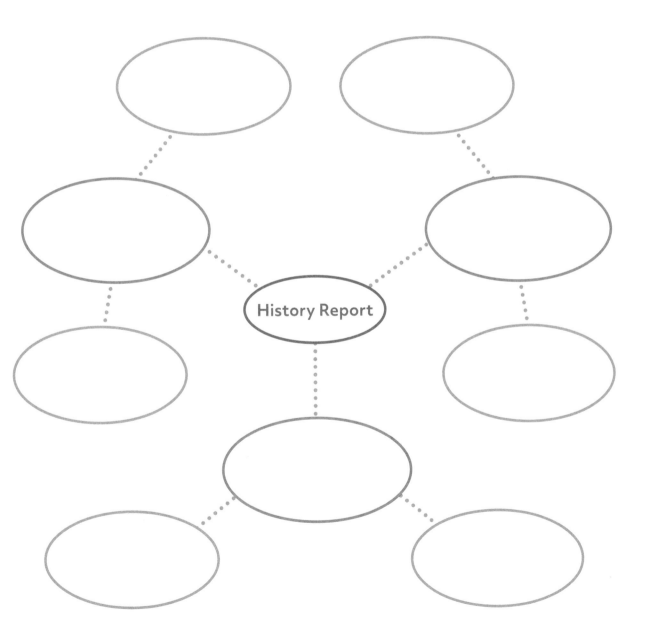

3. Read your topics. Cross off topics that seem too large or broad to cover. Cross off topics that are too small or narrow.

4. Circle any topics that you really would like to write about. If you did not circle any topics, add a few more.

5. Choose your favorite topic that you circled. Then answer Yes or No to each question.

   a. Is the topic focused enough to cover in detail in five paragraphs?

   _____

   b. Is the topic something you can research using trustworthy sources?

   _____

   c. Is the topic interesting to you? _____

6. Did you answer Yes to Parts A–C of Question 5? You have found a topic! If not, go back and complete Question 5 with another topic you named. Repeat until you find a topic that works.

My history report topic is _____.

I can't wait to learn more about my topic!

Informational Writing: Prewriting (B)

Spelling List 12 Activity Bank

Circle any words in the box that you did not spell correctly on the pretest. Using your circled words, complete one activity of your choice. Complete as much of the activity as you can in the time given.

If you spelled all words correctly on the pretest, complete your chosen activity with as many spelling words as you can.

baboon	inconclusive	mousse	tractor	midmorning
droop	mushroom	distract	retract	midriff
exclude	raccoon	subtract	Illinois	midweek
fluent	rude	traction	Wyoming	midtown
acoustic				

Spelling Activity Choices

Create a Crossword

1. Write a word from your spelling word list in the center of the grid paper.

2. Write another spelling word going across and sharing a letter with the first word. See how many words you can connect.

   Example:

			p			
		k	i	s	s	e	s
	d		n			
r	o	c	k	s		
	g					
	s					

Word Search Puzzle

1. Draw a box on the grid paper. The box should be large enough to hold your words from the spelling word list.

2. Fill in the grid paper with words from your spelling list, writing them horizontally, vertically, and diagonally (forward or backward if you choose).

3. Fill in the rest of the box with random letters.

4. Ask someone to find and circle your spelling words in the puzzle you made.

Complete the activity that you chose.

My chosen activity: _____

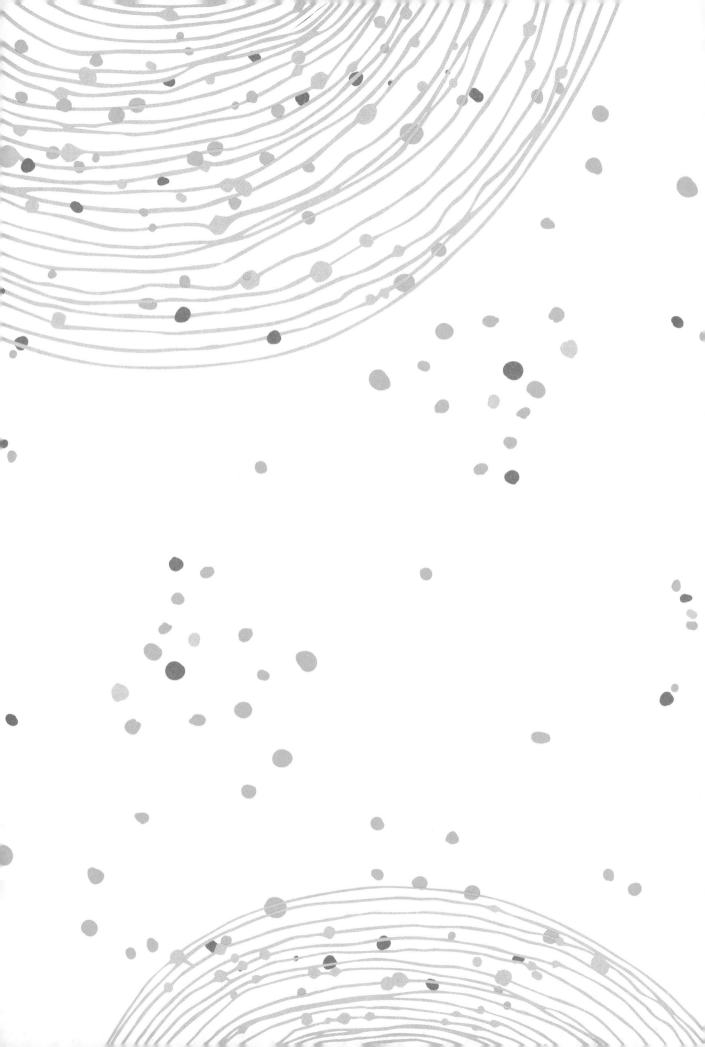

Informational Writing: Prewriting (B)

Conduct Research for Your History Report

Follow these steps to write a research question.

1. A research question is the question that you will answer in your history report. Write three possible research questions for your history report.

    a. _____

    b. _____

    c. _____

2. Choose the research question that most interests you. Be sure that the question is one that you can answer in a five-paragraph report.

    My research question: _____

Follow these steps to conduct research. Record information on the Research Notes pages that follow. Use one page per source.

3. Identify at least two sources. Record the title, author, publisher, and URL of each source.
    - One source must be a print source, such as a book, an article originally published in a newspaper or magazine, or an encyclopedia article.
    - One source must be a digital source found on the Internet.

4. As you read each source, take notes related to your research question.
    - Write your notes in your own words.
    - If you find a direct quotation that you think you might use in your report, record the quotation, word for word, in quotation marks. Also record the name of the person you are quoting.

Research Notes

Source

Title: _____

Author: _____

Published by: _____

URL (if necessary): _____

Notes

Key Information Written in Your Own Words:

_____

_____

_____

_____

_____

_____

Direct Quotation:

_____

_____

_____

Person Quoted: _____

Research Notes

Source

Title: _____

Author: _____

Published by: _____

URL (if necessary): _____

Notes

Key Information Written in Your Own Words:

_____

_____

_____

_____

_____

_____

_____

Direct Quotation:

_____

_____

_____

Person Quoted: _____

Research Notes

Source

Title: _____

Author: _____

Published by: _____

URL (if necessary): _____

Notes

Key Information Written in Your Own Words:

_____

_____

_____

_____

_____

_____

_____

Direct Quotation:

_____

_____

_____

Person Quoted: _____

Informational Writing: Prewriting (C)

Prewriting Your History Report

Use your research notes to complete a graphic organizer for your history report. You do not need to use complete sentences in your graphic organizer.

Note: Your report must include at least one direct quotation and one piece of media, such as a picture, chart, or video clip. So, you only need to fill in one blank labeled "Direct Quotation" and one blank labeled "Possible Use of Media" in your graphic organizer.

Report Title _____

Introduction

Hook: _____

Background: _____

_____

_____

_____

Thesis Statement: _____

_____

Body Paragraph 1

Subtopic: _____

Related Information/Details: _____

_____

_____

_____

_____

Direct Quotation (if appropriate): _____

Image or Media (if appropriate): _____

Body Paragraph 2

Subtopic: _____

Related Information/Details: _____

_____

_____

_____

_____

Direct Quotation (if appropriate): _____

Image or Media (if appropriate): _____

Body Paragraph 3

Subtopic: _____

Related Information/Details: _____

_____

_____

_____

_____

Direct Quotation (if appropriate): _____

Image or Media (if appropriate): _____

Conclusion

Brief Restatement of Thesis: _____

_____

Short Summary of Key Points: _____

_____

_____

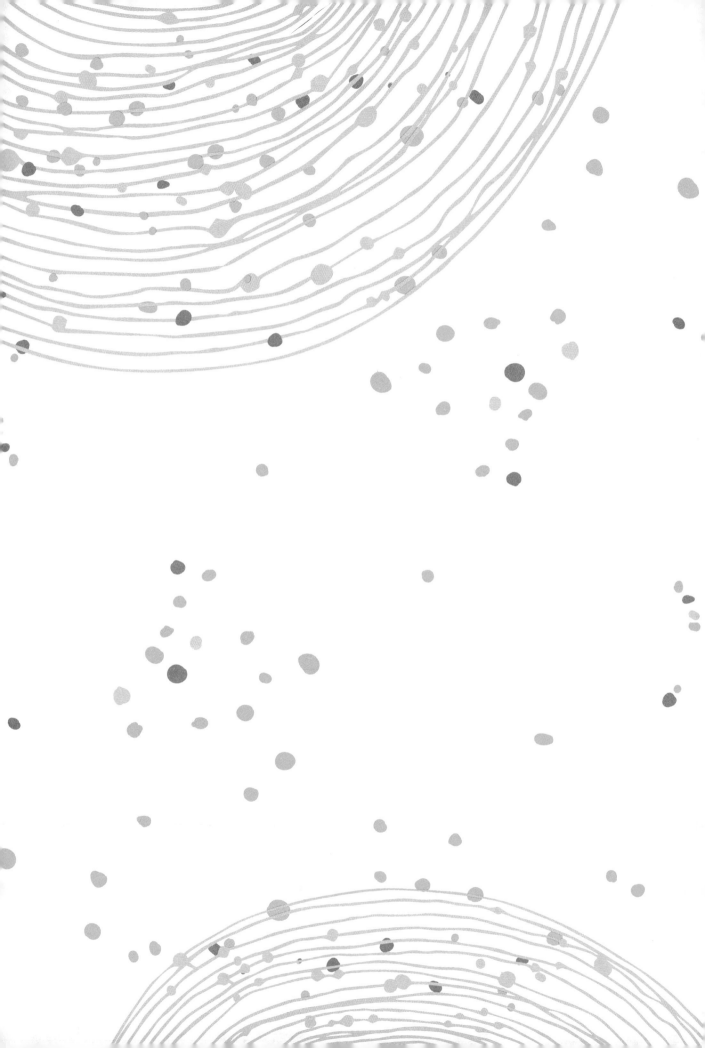

Informational Writing: Drafting (A)

Draft Your History Report

Using your notes and your graphic organizer to guide you, write the first draft of your history report. Write only on the white rows. You will use the purple rows for revisions later.

Title

start here ►

keep writing ►

Draft Page 1

keep writing ▶

Draft Page 2

keep writing ▶

Draft Page 3

keep writing ►

Draft Page 4

Draft Page 5

Draft Page 6

Metaphors

Apply: Metaphors

Answer the questions in complete sentences. In each response, use the metaphor that the question is asking about, and include enough information for a reader to understand the metaphor.

1. What is something that is a *piece of cake* for you?

_____

_____

_____

_____

_____

_____

2. Who do you know that are *two peas in a pod*?

_____

_____

_____

_____

_____

_____

3. Describe someone who is your *sunshine*.

_____

_____

_____

_____

_____

_____

4. Who do you know that is a *night owl*?

_____

_____

_____

_____

_____

_____

Poetry (A)

Spelling List 13 Pretest

1. Open the Spelling Pretest activity online. Listen to the first spelling word. Type the word. Check your answer.

2. Write the correct spelling of the word in the Word column of the Spelling Pretest table on the next page.

Word	✓	✗
1 blindfold		

3. Put a check mark in the ✓ column if you spelled the word correctly online.

Word	✓	✗
1 blindfold	✓	

Put an X in the ✗ column if you spelled the word incorrectly online.

Word	✓	✗
1 blindfold		✗

4. Repeat Steps 1–3 for the remaining words in the Spelling Pretest.

Poetry (A)

Spelling List 13 Pretest

Write each spelling word in the Word column, making sure to spell it correctly.

	Word	✓	✗
1			
2			
3			
4			
5			
6			
7			
8			
9			

	Word	✓	✗
10			
11			
12			
13			
14			
15			
16			
17			

Write a Summary of a Poem

Write your response in complete sentences.

Write a summary of the poem "The Ecchoing Green." Be sure to include the most important information from each stanza. Also include the theme of the poem.

_____

_____

_____

_____

_____

_____

_____

_____

_____

_____

_____

_____

_____

_____

_____

_____

_____

_____

Poetry (B)

Spelling List 13 Activity Bank

Circle any words in the box that you did not spell correctly on the pretest. Using your circled words, complete one activity of your choice. Complete as much of the activity as you can in the time given.

If you spelled all words correctly on the pretest, complete your chosen activity with as many spelling words as you can.

absurd	shirt	figure	research	earning
concern	misery	survive	mockingbird	Alaska
disturb	observe	thirsty	unlearn	Vermont
firm	pearl			

Spelling Activity Choices

Vowel-Free Words

1. In the left column, write only the consonants in each word and put a dot where each vowel should be.

2. Spell each word out loud, stating which vowels should be in the places you wrote dots.

3. In the right column, rewrite the entire spelling word.

4. Correct any spelling errors.

Alphabetizing

1. In the left column, write your words from the spelling word list in alphabetical order.

2. Correct any spelling errors.

Parts of Speech

1. In the left column, write the words from your spelling list that are nouns.

2. In the right column, write all the other words from your spelling list and label each word's part of speech.

3. Correct any spelling errors.

Uppercase and Lowercase

1. In the left column, write each of your words in all capital letters, or all uppercase.

2. In the right column, write each of your words in all lowercase letters.

3. Correct any spelling errors.

Complete the activity that you chose.

My chosen activity: _____

1. _____   _____
2. _____   _____
3. _____   _____
4. _____   _____
5. _____   _____
6. _____   _____
7. _____   _____
8. _____   _____
9. _____   _____
10. _____   _____
11. _____   _____
12. _____   _____
13. _____   _____
14. _____   _____
15. _____   _____
16. _____   _____
17. _____   _____
18. _____   _____
19. _____   _____
20. _____   _____
21. _____   _____
22. _____   _____
23. _____   _____
24. _____   _____
25. _____   _____

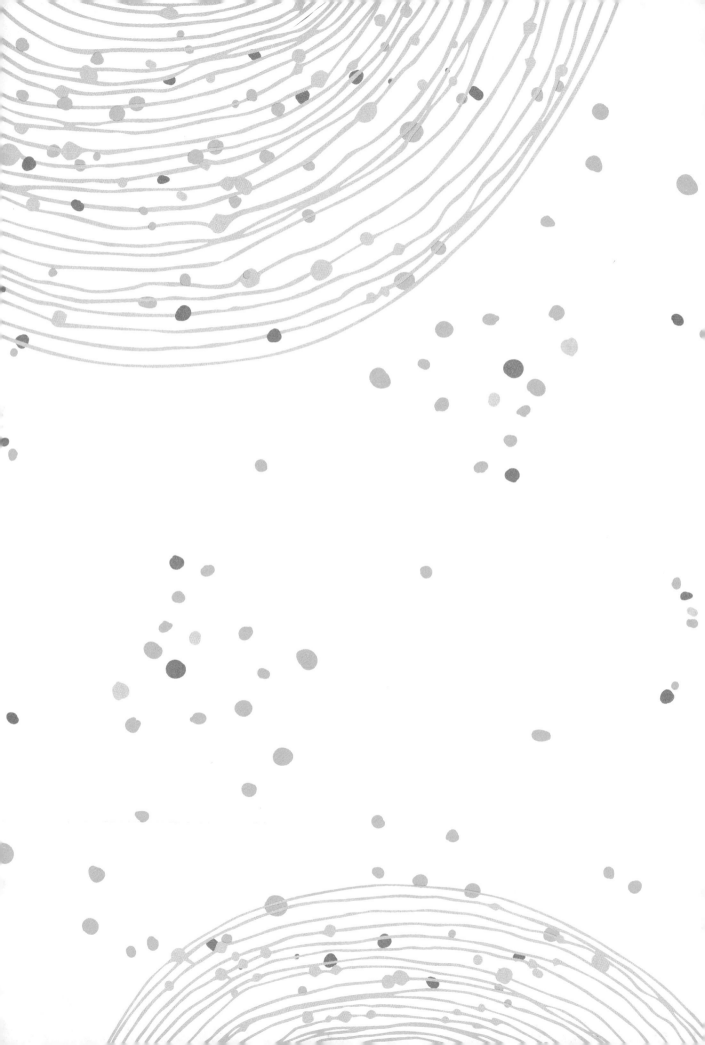

Poetry (B)

Write Poetry into Prose

Write your response in complete sentences.

Write a prose version of the poem "Bed in Summer."

In northern Alaska, it stays light nearly 24 hours a day in the summer.

Poetry (C)

Write a Found Narrative Poem

Write your own found narrative poem.

1. Choose a narrative story. It can be a narrative that you have written or one that you have read. Write your story's title:

2. Use the graphic organizer to plan your poem.

   a. Write one sentence each to describe the beginning, the middle, and the end of the narrative.

   b. Record words and phrases from the narrative that show the beginning, the middle, and the end. You can also add your own details.

> Beginning

↓

> Middle

↓

> End

3. Write your found narrative poem. Make sure your poem

- Is at least three stanzas long
- Tells a narrative with a beginning, middle, and end
- Includes sensory details and figurative language
- Has at least two structural elements, such as rhyme, rhythm, and meter

start here ▶

keep writing ▶

Draft Page 1

4. Read your poem aloud. Use the items in Question 3 as a checklist to revise your poem.

5. Write a final copy of your poem.

Poetry Wrap-Up

Write About Your Favorite Poem

Poems may make us think about things we have experienced or books we have read. They may make us think about the world around us.

Which poem did **you** connect with the most? Why?

- "The Ecchoing Green" by William Blake
- "Try, Try Again" by William Edward Hickson
- "Wynken, Blyken, and Nod" by Eugene Field
- "Bed in Summer" by Robert Louis Stevenson

Informational Writing: Revising

Revise Your History Report

Use the checklist as you revise your history report draft.

Organization

☐ Does my report have an introduction, at least three body paragraphs, and a conclusion?

☐ Does my introduction clearly state the topic?

☐ Are supporting ideas grouped in the correct body paragraphs?

☐ Do appropriate headings separate the different sections of my report?

☐ Do I use clear and logical transitions?

Content

☐ Is my report factual and well researched, showing that I understand the topic?

☐ Do I use enough facts and supporting details, including at least one quotation, to explain ideas?

☐ Does my conclusion make sense and answer important questions?

☐ Are the words I use precise and domain-specific?

☐ Do I have a source list that includes at least two research sources, one print and one digital?

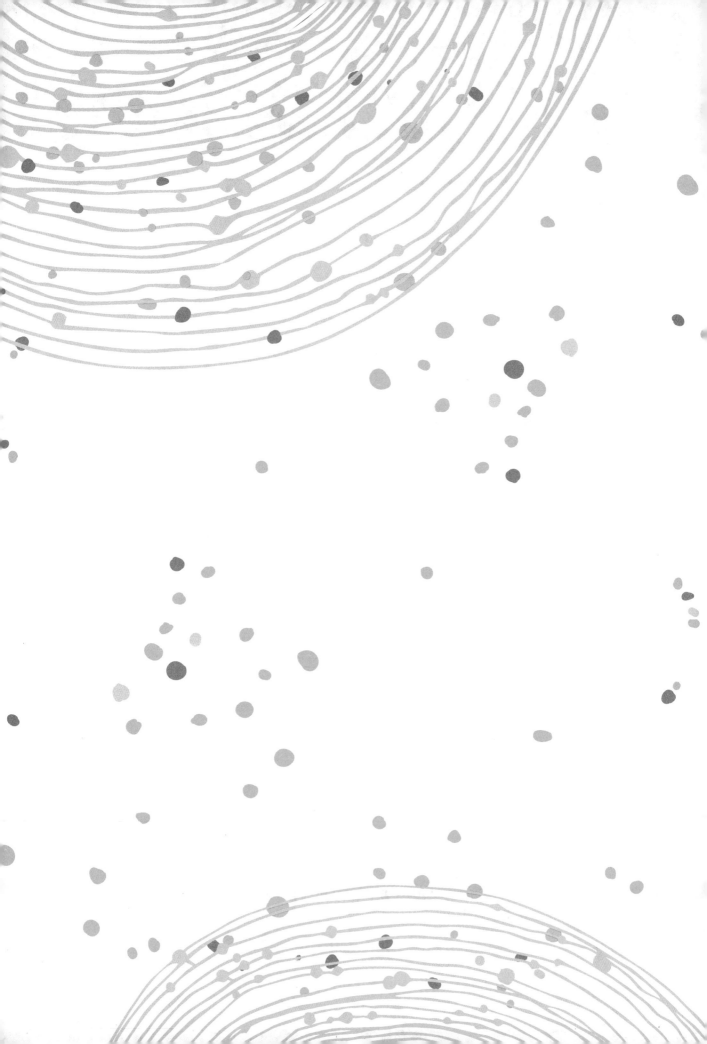

Informational Writing: Proofreading

Proofread Your History Report

Use the checklist as you proofread your history report draft.

Grammar and Usage

☐ Are all sentences complete and correct?

☐ Are there any missing or extra words?

☐ Are all verbs in the appropriate tense?

☐ Are there other grammatical or usage errors?

Mechanics

☐ Is every word spelled correctly, including frequently confused words?

☐ Does every sentence begin with a capital letter and end with the appropriate punctuation?

☐ Are proper nouns and adjectives capitalized?

☐ Are direct quotations punctuated correctly?

☐ Are titles of works capitalized correctly?

☐ Are there other punctuation or capitalization errors?

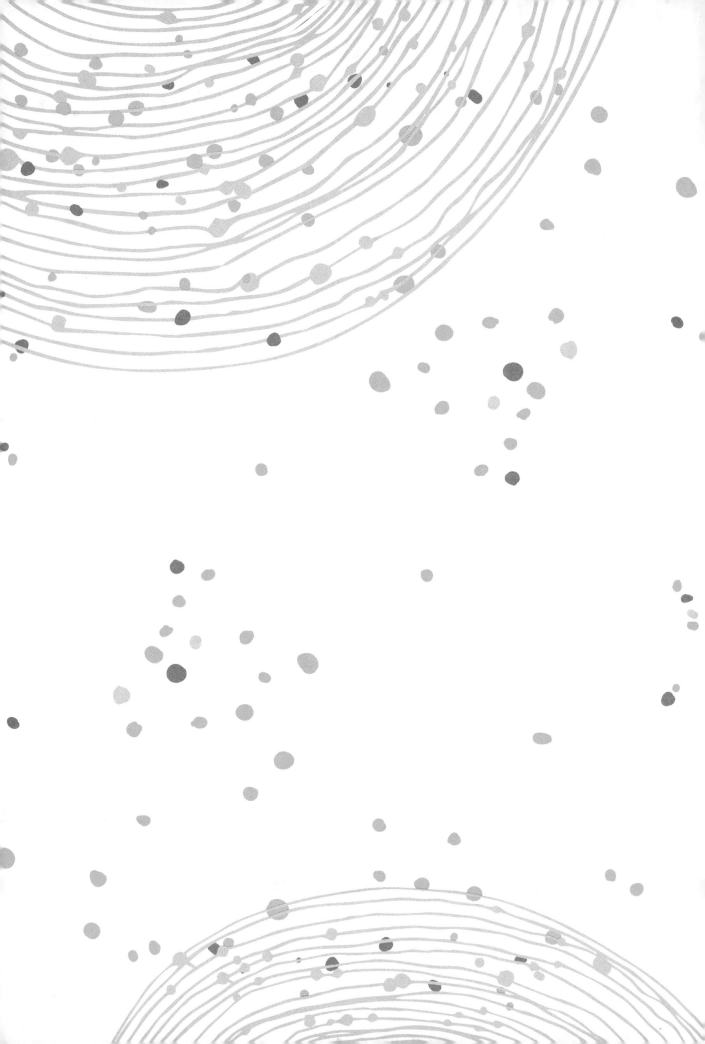

"Rikki-Tikki-Tavi" (A)

Spelling List 14 Pretest

1. Open the Spelling Pretest activity online. Listen to the first spelling word. Type the word. Check your answer.

2. Write the correct spelling of the word in the Word column of the Spelling Pretest table on the next page.

Word	✓	✗
1 blindfold		

3. Put a check mark in the ✓ column if you spelled the word correctly online.

Word	✓	✗
1 blindfold	✓	

   Put an X in the ✗ column if you spelled the word incorrectly online.

Word	✓	✗
1 blindfold		X

4. Repeat Steps 1–3 for the remaining words in the Spelling Pretest.

"Rikki-Tikki-Tavi" (A)

Spelling List 14 Pretest

Write each spelling word in the Word column, making sure to spell it correctly.

	Word	✓	✗
1			
2			
3			
4			
5			
6			
7			
8			
9			

	Word	✓	✗
10			
11			
12			
13			
14			
15			
16			
17			

"Rikki-Tikki-Tavi" (A)

Write About a True Mongoose

In Chapter 1 of "Rikki-Tikki-Tavi," Rudyard Kipling calls Rikki-tikki a "true mongoose." Underline any phrases that describe a "true mongoose" in the excerpt.

It is the hardest thing in the world to frighten a mongoose, because he is eaten up from nose to tail with curiosity. The motto of all the mongoose family is "Run and find out," and Rikki-tikki was a true mongoose. He looked at the cotton wool, decided that it was not good to eat, ran all round the table, sat up and put his fur in order, scratched himself, and jumped on the small boy's shoulder.

"Don't be frightened, Teddy," said his father. "That's his way of making friends."

"Ouch! He's tickling under my chin," said Teddy.

Rikki-tikki looked down between the boy's collar and neck, snuffed at his ear, and climbed down to the floor, where he sat rubbing his nose.

"Good gracious," said Teddy's mother, "and that's a wild creature! I suppose he's so tame because we've been kind to him."

"All mongooses are like that," said her husband. "If Teddy doesn't pick him up by the tail, or try to put him in a cage, he'll run in and out of the house all day long. Let's give him something to eat."

They gave him a little piece of raw meat. Rikki-tikki liked it immensely, and when it was finished he went out into the veranda and sat in the sunshine and fluffed up his fur to make it dry to the roots. Then he felt better.

"There are more things to find out about in this house," he said to himself, "than all my family could find out in all their lives. I shall certainly stay and find out."

He spent all that day roaming over the house. He nearly drowned himself in the bathtub, put his nose into the ink on a writing table, and burned it on the end of the big man's cigar, for he climbed up in the big man's lap to see how writing was done. At nightfall he ran into Teddy's nursery to watch how kerosene lamps were lighted, and when Teddy went to bed Rikki-tikki climbed up too.

But he was a restless companion, because he had to get up and attend to every noise all through the night, and find out what made it. Teddy's mother and father came in, the last thing, to look at their boy, and Rikki-tikki was awake on the pillow.

"I don't like that," said Teddy's mother. "He may bite the child."

"He'll do no such thing," said the father. "Teddy's safer with that little beast than if he had a bloodhound to watch him. If a snake came into the nursery now—"

Write a paragraph that gives two or more reasons why Rikki-tikki is a "true mongoose." When you finish, illustrate your paragraph.

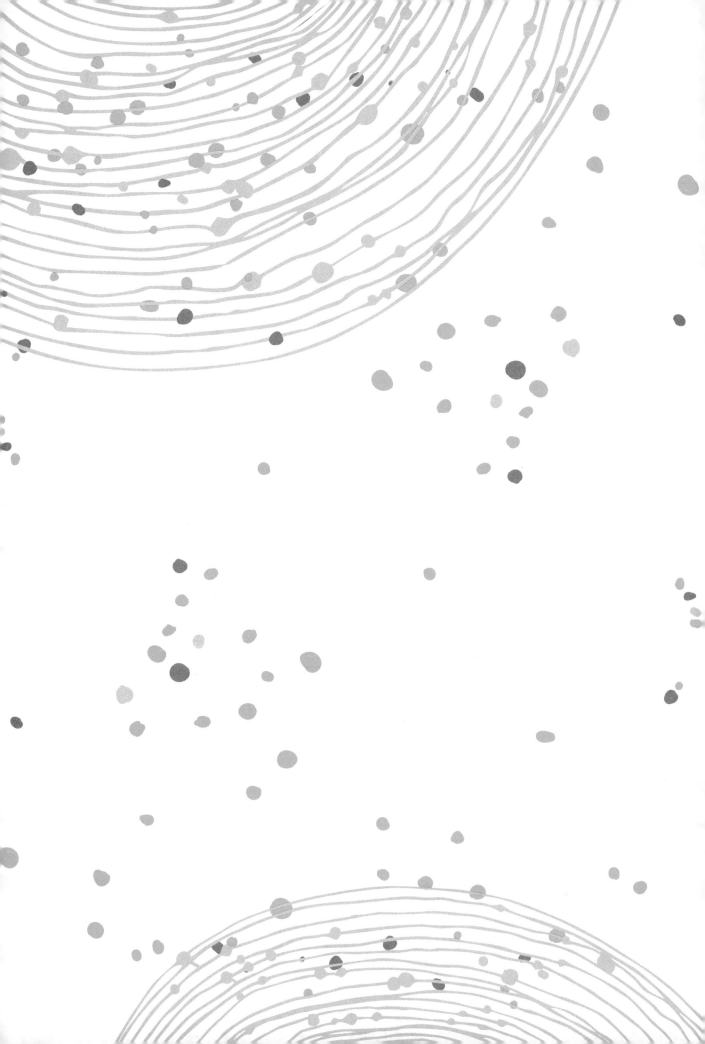

"Rikki-Tikki-Tavi" (B)

Spelling List 14 Activity Bank

Circle any words in the box that you did not spell correctly on the pretest. Using your circled words, complete one activity of your choice. Complete as much of the activity as you can in the time given.

If you spelled all words correctly on the pretest, complete your chosen activity with as many spelling words as you can.

ache	chorus	package	invisible	vista
arctic	mechanic	skeleton	visible	Colorado
campus	speckled	stomach	vision	Montana
character	octopus			

Spelling Activity Choices

Silly Sentences

1. Write a silly sentence using your words from the spelling word list.

2. Underline the spelling word in each sentence.
   Example: The dog was <u>driving</u> a car.

3. Correct any spelling errors.

Spelling Story

1. Write a very short story using your words from the spelling word list.

2. Underline the spelling words in the story.

3. Correct any spelling errors.

Riddle Me This

1. Write a riddle for your words from the spelling word list.
   Example: "I have a trunk, but it's not on my car."

2. Write the answer, which is your word, for each riddle.
   Example: Answer: elephant

3. Correct any spelling errors.

RunOnWord

1. Gather some crayons, colored pencils, or markers. Write each of your words, using a different color for each word, end to end as one long word.
   Example: dogcatbirdfishturtle

2. Rewrite the words correctly and with proper spacing.

Complete the activity that you chose.

My chosen activity: _____

_____

_____

_____

_____

_____

_____

_____

_____

_____

_____

_____

_____

_____

_____

_____

_____

_____

_____

_____

_____

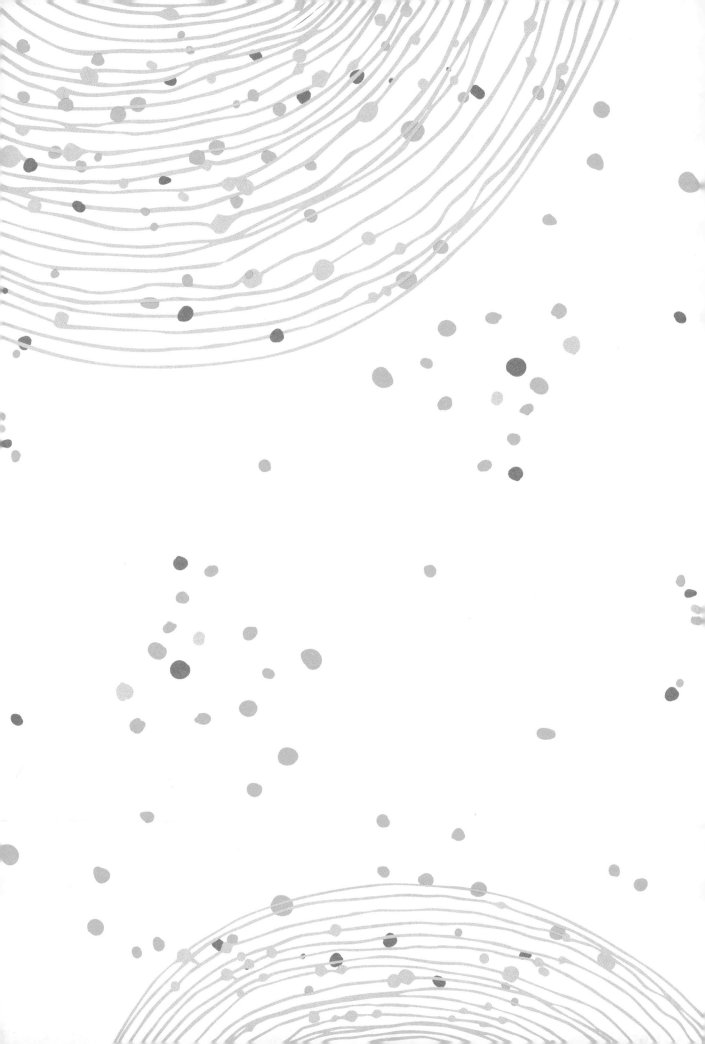

"Rikki-Tikki-Tavi" (B)

Write About Author's Word Choice in "Rikki-Tikki-Tavi"

Read the excerpt from "Rikki-Tikki-Tavi" by Rudyard Kipling.

Rikki-tikki knew better than to waste time in staring. He jumped up in the air as high as he could go, and just under him whizzed by the head of Nagaina, Nag's wicked wife. She had crept up behind him as he was talking, to make an end of him. He heard her savage hiss as the stroke missed.

He came down almost across her back, and if he had been an old mongoose he would have known that then was the time to break her back with one bite. But he was afraid of the terrible lashing return stroke of the cobra. He bit, indeed, but did not bite long enough, and he jumped clear of the whisking tail, leaving Nagaina torn and angry.

What if the author had used different words to describe Nagaina? How does the phrase "Nag's wicked wife" compare to "Nag's mean wife" or "Nag's angry wife"? Write your answer.

Today, *wicked* means
excellent. What would
Kipling think of that?

"Rikki-Tikki-Tavi"(C)

Write About Comparing Versions of a Story

Think about a time you watched a movie based on a book. What was the title? Which version did you like better, the movie or the book? Write three reasons to explain your answer.

_____

_____

_____

_____

_____

_____

_____

_____

_____

_____

_____

_____

_____

_____

_____

_____

_____

_____

_____

_____

_____

_____

_____

_____

_____

"Rikki-Tikki-Tavi" Wrap-Up

Write About Important Events in "Rikki-Tikki-Tavi"

What do you think is the most important thing that happens in the story "Rikki-Tikki-Tavi"? How would the story change if this event did not occur? Write your answer.

Latin Roots

Apply: Latin Roots

For each item, choose the word that best fills in the blank and explain your choice. Think about the context clues and what they suggest about the missing word. Use complete sentences when you explain your choice.

1. When I visit Hawaii, I spend a lot of time snorkeling. There is a large variety of _____ life on and around the coral reefs. There are crabs, eels, sea turtles, sea stars, and very colorful fish. If you're lucky, you even see dolphins.

   Would you choose *submarine* or *marine* to fill the blank? Why?

   _____

   _____

2. At the game, the crowd was very _____ . The cheerleaders got everybody on their feet clapping and cheering for the home team. Everyone had a lot of energy. They really got excited when the home team scored.

   Would you choose *animated* or *inanimate* to fill the blank? Why?

   _____

   _____

3. Many people study animals that live deep in the ocean. But they have to use a special _____ to get to the bottom of the sea. They need a vessel that can handle the pressure of the ocean depths.

Would you choose *submarine* or *marine* to fill the blank? Why?

_____

_____

Can an animator animate an inanimate object?

Quilting (A)

Spelling List 15 Pretest

1. Open the Spelling Pretest activity online. Listen to the first spelling word. Type the word. Check your answer.

2. Write the correct spelling of the word in the Word column of the Spelling Pretest table on the next page.

Word	✓	✗
1 blindfold		

3. Put a check mark in the ✓ column if you spelled the word correctly online.

Word	✓	✗
1 blindfold	✓	

Put an X in the ✗ column if you spelled the word incorrectly online.

Word	✓	✗
1 blindfold		X

4. Repeat Steps 1–3 for the remaining words in the Spelling Pretest.

Quilting (A)

Spelling List 15 Pretest

Write each spelling word in the Word column, making sure to spell it correctly.

	Word	✓	✗
1			
2			
3			
4			
5			
6			
7			
8			
9			
10			
11			
12			
13			

	Word	✓	✗
14			
15			
16			
17			
18			
19			
20			
21			
22			
23			
24			
25			

Quilting (A)

How Do You Do That?

You have read the sequence of steps for making a quilt. Now, write the sequence of steps for making or doing something else. Use complete sentences in your response.

Choose between making toast or brushing your teeth. OR, choose your own action. Write the sequence of steps for completing one of these actions. You may write the steps in a paragraph, like in *The Quilting Bee*, or you may write numbered steps.

_____

_____

_____

_____

_____

_____

_____

_____

_____

_____

_____

_____

_____

_____

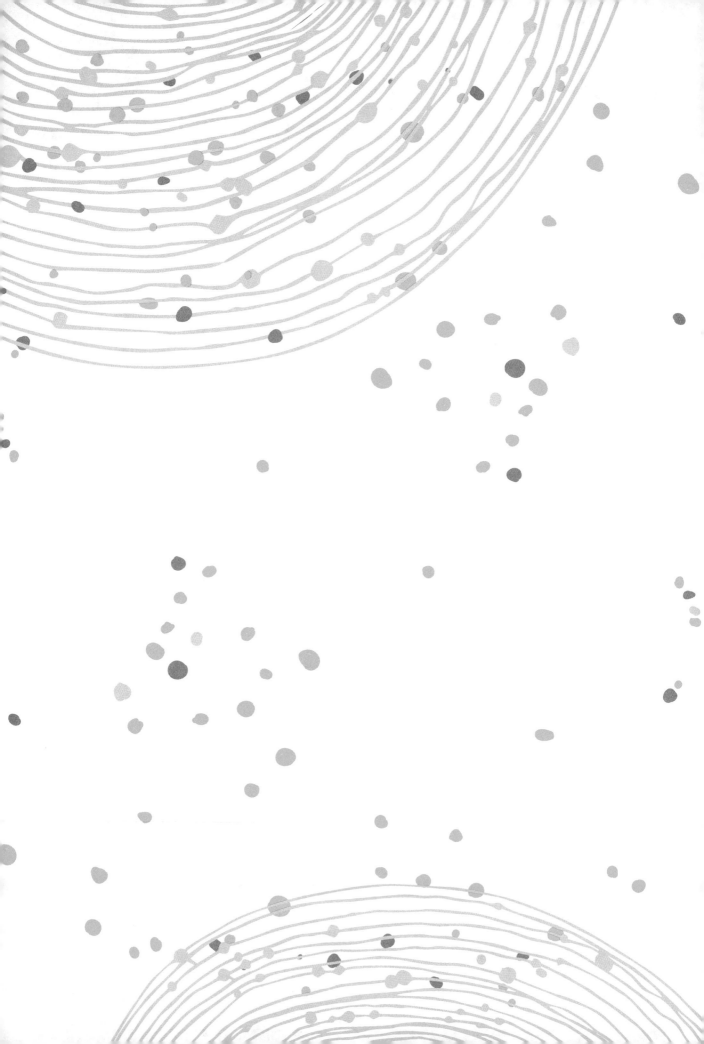

Quilting (B)

Spelling List 15 Activity Bank

Circle any words in the box that you did not spell correctly on the pretest. Using your circled words, complete one activity of your choice. Complete as much of the activity as you can in the time given.

If you spelled all words correctly on the pretest, complete your chosen activity with as many spelling words as you can.

artificial	quiet	financial	concur	Mississippi
official	quotation	equal	current	declaw
social	squirrel	questions	cursive	deface
commercial	facial	squid	recur	defrost
quarterly	crucial	aqua	Arizona	dethrone

Spelling Activity Choices

Hidden Words

1. Draw a picture and "hide" as many words from the Spelling Word List inside the picture as you can.

2. See if others can find the words within the picture.

Triangle Spelling

Write each word in a triangle.

Ghost Words

1. Use a white crayon to write each spelling word.

2. Go over the white crayon writing with a colored marker.

Complete the activity that you chose.

My chosen activity: _____

Quilting (B)

Write a Summary of *Sweet Clara and the Freedom Quilt*

Write your response in complete sentences.

Write a summary of *Sweet Clara and the Freedom Quilt*. The summary should include the main characters, the setting, and the most important details and events. Remember that your summary should describe the events in the order they happen in the story.

_____

_____

_____

_____

_____

_____

_____

_____

_____

_____

_____

_____

_____

_____

_____

_____

_____

I wonder what amazing stories are part of my family's history.

Quilting (C)

Write About Illustrations

Answer the questions. Use complete sentences in your answers.

1. In the illustrations, the author only uses color for Anna's clothes that are used to make the quilt, and then the quilt itself. How does the color in the illustrations help tell the story?

_____

_____

_____

_____

_____

_____

_____

2. Gather drawing and coloring tools such as crayons, pencils, and markers. Use the empty square to illustrate a quilt square that shows things that are important in your life.

3. What does the quilt square mean to you?

_____

_____

_____

_____

_____

_____

_____

Make a Family Tree

The Keeping Quilt is a story in which we can see how the past influences the future. The family's past generations are connected to future generations through the family's quilt and family traditions. Answer the questions, and then fill in a family tree that shows how the members of the author's family are related to each other.

1. How is the author of the story, Patricia Polacco, connected to past generations of her family and their traditions? Give at least two examples supported by details from the story.

_____

_____

_____

_____

_____

_____

_____

_____

_____

_____

2. Who does Anna marry?

_____

3. Who is Anna's daughter? Who does Anna's daughter marry?

_____

4. Who is Carle's daughter?

_____

5. Who is Mary Ellen's daughter?

_____

6. Who are Patricia's children?

_____

7. Complete the family tree showing how each generation is connected to the other generations. Anna and Traci have been placed in the tree to help you get started.

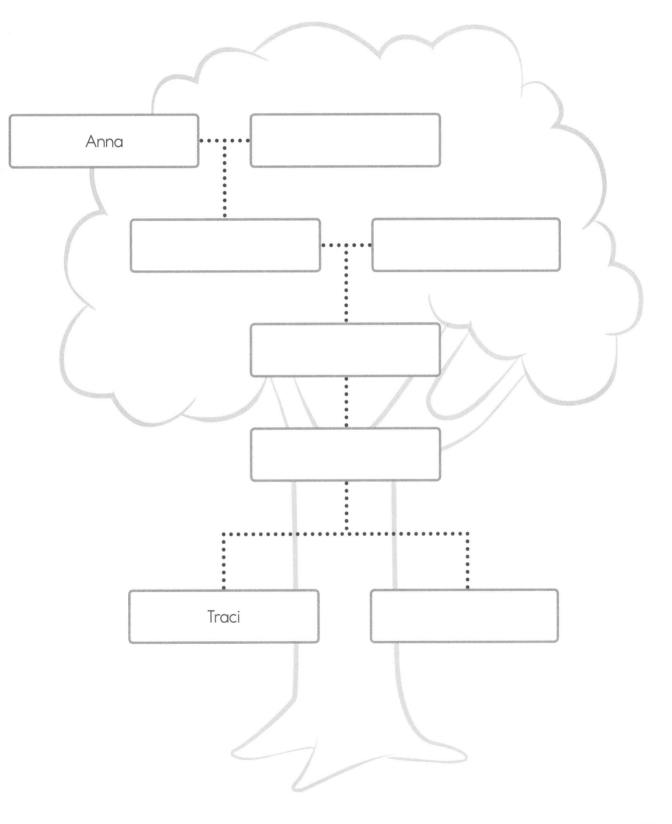

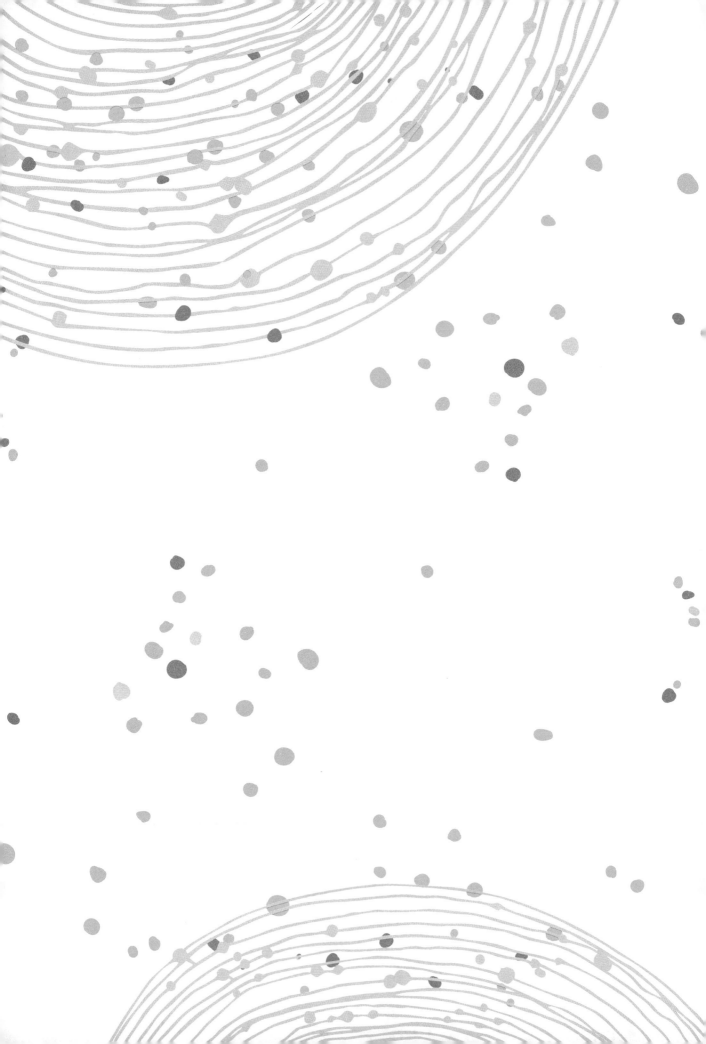

Quilting (E)

What's the Same? What's Different?

Choose one of the fiction stories to compare with the nonfiction text *The Quilting Bee.* Then answer the questions to compare or contrast the fiction and nonfiction texts. Use complete sentences in your answers.

1. Circle the title of the book you will compare/contrast with *The Quilting Bee.*

   Sweet Clara and the Freedom Quilt   **The Keeping Quilt**

2. Is the point of view in the books the same or different? Explain.

   _____

   _____

   _____

   _____

   _____

   _____

   _____

3. What is the same or different about the illustrations?

   _____

   _____

   _____

   _____

4. What do the illustrations draw attention to in each story? Give an example from each book.

_____

_____

_____

_____

_____

_____

_____

_____

_____

_____

_____

_____

_____

5. Is the reason for making the quilt the same or different in each book? Explain the reason for making the quilt in each story.

_____

_____

_____

_____

_____

_____

_____

Quilting Wrap-Up

Write About Quilts and History

Answer the questions. Use complete sentences in your answers.

1. How do historical events influence the author's choices of characters, setting, and plot in *Sweet Clara and the Freedom Quilt*?

2. How is history a part of the book *The Quilting Bee*?

3. What is different about how history is a part of *The Quilting Bee* and
   Sweet Clara and the Freedom Quilt?

   _____

   _____

   _____

   _____

   _____

   _____

   _____

4. Does any historical event influence the story of *The Keeping Quilt*?
   Explain.

   _____

   _____

   _____

   _____

   _____

   _____

   _____

5. What is the same about how history is a part of *The Keeping Quilt* and *Sweet Clara and the Freedom Quilt*?

_____

_____

_____

_____

_____

_____

_____

6. How does the story of *The Keeping Quilt* focus on family history?

_____

_____

_____

_____

_____

_____

_____

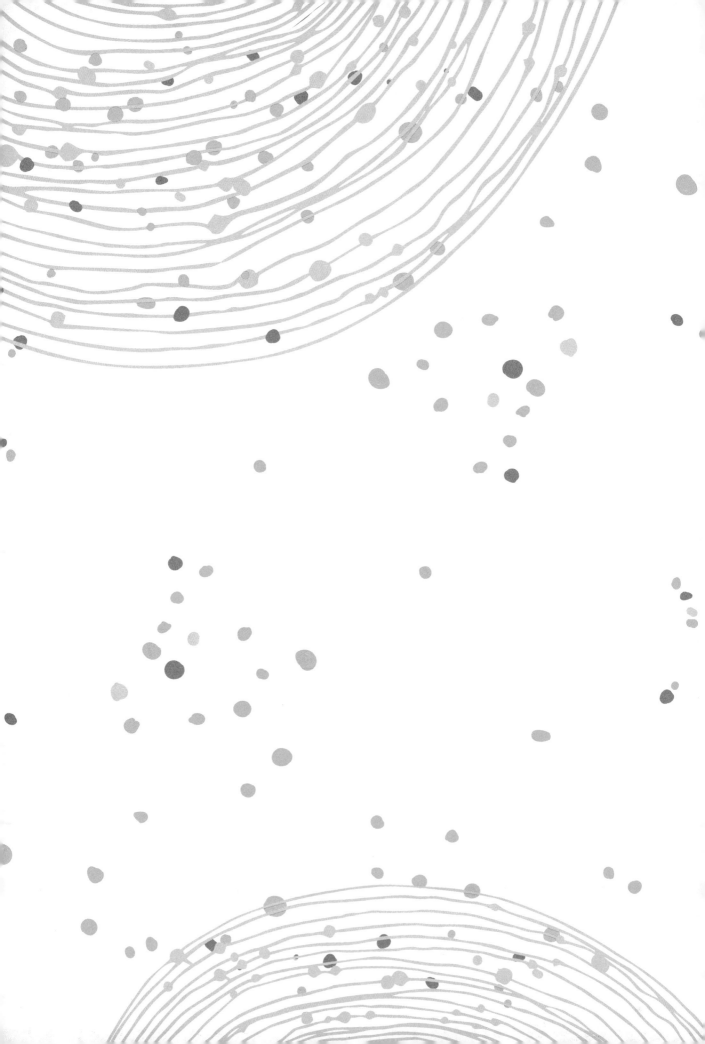

Opinion Writing Skills (A)

Spelling List 16 Pretest

1. Open the Spelling Pretest activity online. Listen to the first spelling word. Type the word. Check your answer.

2. Write the correct spelling of the word in the Word column of the Spelling Pretest table on the next page.

Word	✓	✕
1 blindfold		

3. Put a check mark in the ✓ column if you spelled the word correctly online.

Word	✓	✕
1 blindfold	✓	

Put an X in the ✕ column if you spelled the word incorrectly online.

Word	✓	✕
1 blindfold		✕

4. Repeat Steps 1–3 for the remaining words in the Spelling Pretest.

Opinion Writing Skills (A)

Spelling List 16 Pretest

Write each spelling word in the Word column, making sure to spell it correctly.

	Word	✓	✗
1			
2			
3			
4			
5			
6			
7			
8			
9			

	Word	✓	✗
10			
11			
12			
13			
14			
15			
16			
17			

TRY IT

Opinion Writing Skills (A)

Begin Your Book Review

Use the prompt to answer the questions.

Prompt: **Write a review of a book that you read recently.**

1. Think about the piece you are reviewing.

   a. What is the title of the piece?

   _____

   b. Who is the author?

   _____

   _____

   c. What is the piece about? Summarize the piece in 1 or 2 sentences.

   _____

   _____

   _____

   _____

2. Think about your opinion. Use complete sentences when answering the questions.

   a. What is your opinion of the piece you are reviewing?

   _____

b. How does the piece make you feel?

_____

c. Why do you think and feel this way about the book?

_____

_____

3. Write an introduction to your book review. Use your answers to Questions 1 and 2 to help.

_____

_____

_____

_____

_____

_____

_____

_____

_____

_____

_____

_____

_____

_____

_____

4. Think about how you would organize the remainder of your review. Then complete the outline. Write only one sentence in each box.

Reason 1:

_____

_____

Reason 2:

_____

_____

Reason 3:

_____

_____

Conclusion:

_____

_____

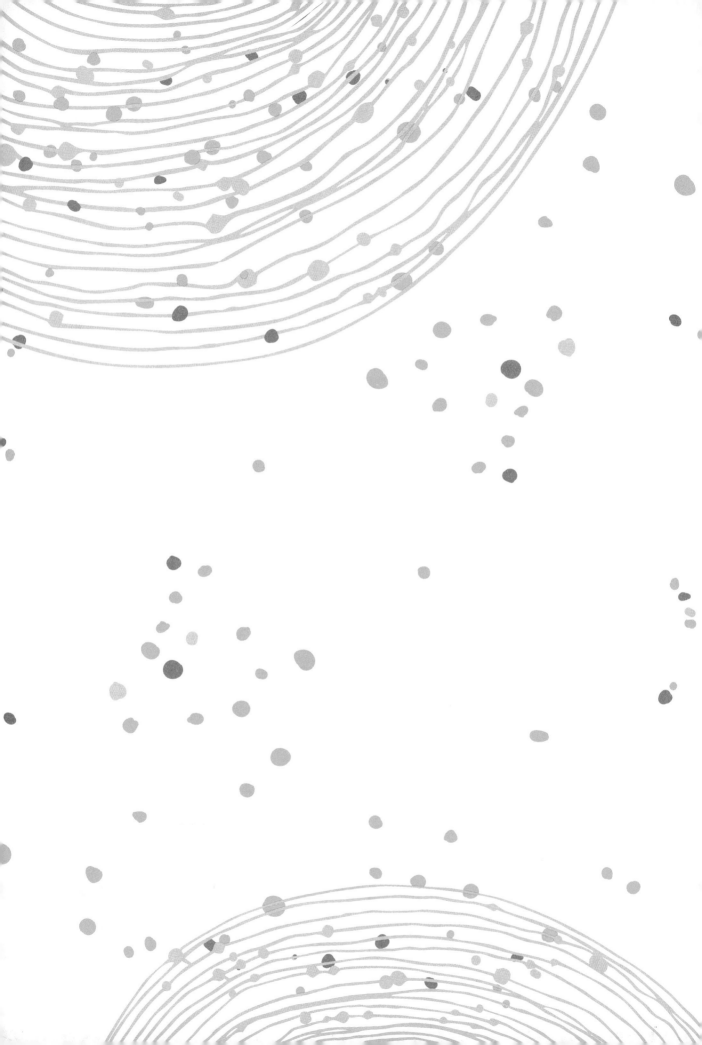

Opinion Writing Skills (B)

Spelling List 16 Activity Bank

Circle any words in the box that you did not spell correctly on the pretest. Using your circled words, complete one activity of your choice. Complete as much of the activity as you can in the time given.

If you spelled all words correctly on the pretest, complete your chosen activity with as many spelling words as you can.

champion	memorial	period	avenue	venture
curiosity	trio	radio	convention	Hawaii
librarian	piano	trivia	vent	Louisiana
machine	patriot			

Spelling Activity Choices

Create a Crossword

1. Write a word from your spelling word list in the center of the grid paper.

2. Write another spelling word going across and sharing a letter with the first word. See how many words you can connect.

Example:

			p			
		k	i	s	s	e	s
	d		n			
r	o	c	k	s		
	g					
	s					

Word Search Puzzle

1. Draw a box on the grid paper. The box should be large enough to hold your words from the spelling word list.

2. Fill in the grid paper with words from your spelling list, writing them horizontally, vertically, and diagonally (forwards or backwards if you choose).

3. Fill in the rest of the box with random letters.

4. Ask someone to find and circle your spelling words in the puzzle you made.

Complete the activity that you chose.

My chosen activity: _____

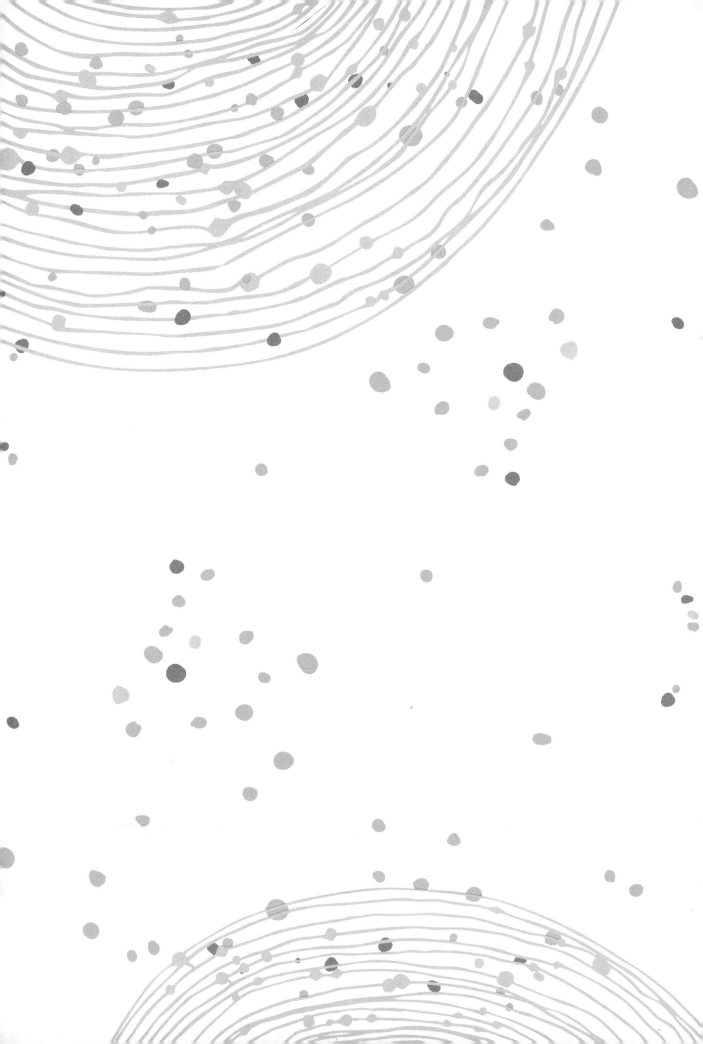

TRY IT

Opinion Writing Skills (B)

Support Reasons in Your Book Review

Use the prompt to complete the graphic organizer.

Prompt: **Write a review of a book that you read recently.**

List your opinion of the piece you are reviewing and three reasons that support your opinion. For each reason, list at least two supporting facts or details.

Opinion:

I think _____

_____

Reason 1:

_____

Supporting facts or details:

- _____

  _____

- _____

  _____

Reason 2:

_____

Supporting facts or details:

- _____

  _____

- _____

  _____

Reason 3:

_____

Supporting facts or details:

- _____

  _____

- _____

  _____

Conclude Your Book Review

Use the prompt to answer the questions.

Prompt: **Write a review of a book that you read recently.**

1. Write one body paragraph of your review.

   a. Look back at your opinion and the first reason that supports it.
   Rewrite the sentence stating your first reason and include a transition
   that connects the reason to your opinion. Some possible transitions
   are *first, the first reason for my opinion, for example,* and *specifically.*
   Underline the transition in your sentence.

   _____

   _____

   _____

   b. Write the remainder of the first body paragraph. Use at least
   one transition to connect your supporting facts and details to the
   reason. Some possible transitions are *for instance, in particular,*
   and *especially.* Underline the transitions in your paragraph.

   _____

   _____

   _____

   _____

   _____

   _____

2. Write the conclusion to your review.

- Start with a transition, such as *To sum it up*, *In conclusion*, *All in all*, or *As you can see*.

- State your opinion in words that are different from what you wrote in your introduction.

- Briefly remind readers of your reasons.

- State who would most like to read the piece you are writing about.

_____

_____

_____

_____

_____

_____

_____

_____

_____

Tell a friend about your favorite book!

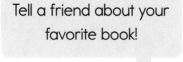

Opinion Writing Skills Wrap-Up

Use Opinion Writing Skills

Use the graphic organizer to answer the questions.

1. Write an opinion paragraph about your favorite dessert.

   a. In the top scoop, complete the sentence to state your opinion.

   b. In the bottom scoop, write one reason for your opinion. Support your reason with at least one fact and one detail.

   c. In the cone, complete the sentence to conclude your paragraph. Your conclusion should summarize your opinion and reason.

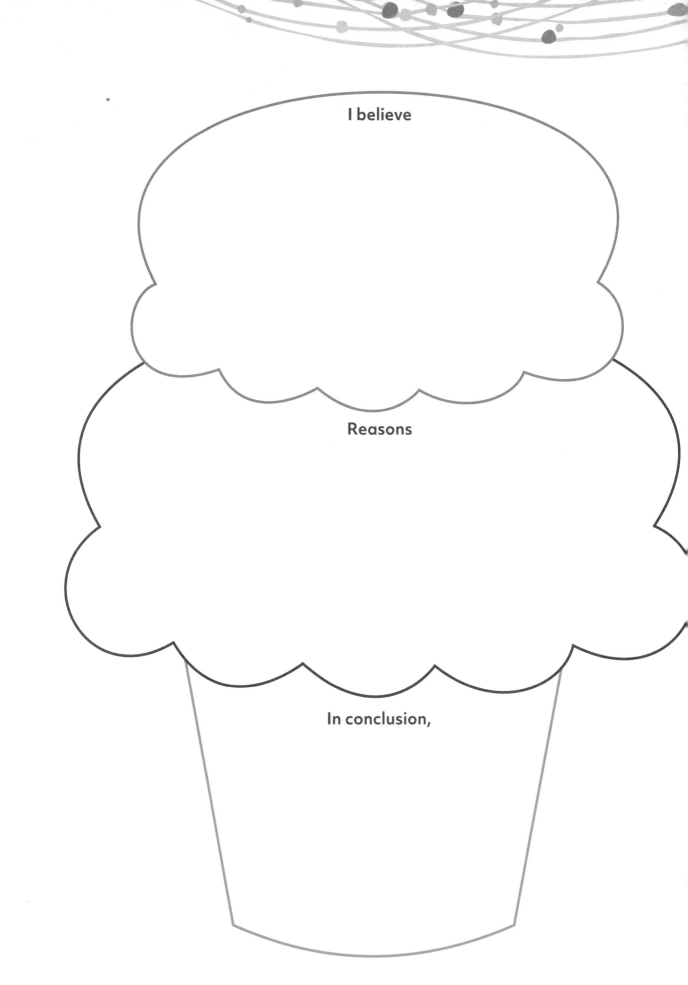

I believe

Reasons

In conclusion,

2. Introducing a topic is an important part of an introduction.

Look back at your introductory sentence. Imagine that someone reading that sentence has never seen, tasted, or smelled your dessert. Revise your introduction to include more detail. You can revise your introductory sentence or add a second sentence.

Revised introduction:

_____

_____

_____

3. Strong writers provide facts and details to support their reasons.

a. Underline at least one fact you used to support your reason. If necessary, write a fact:

_____

_____

b. Circle at least one detail you used to support your reason. If necessary, write a detail:

_____

_____

4. Strong writers use transitions to connect reasons to an opinion.

Underline the transition that connects your reason to your opinion. If necessary, rewrite the sentence that states your reason to include a transition:

_____

_____

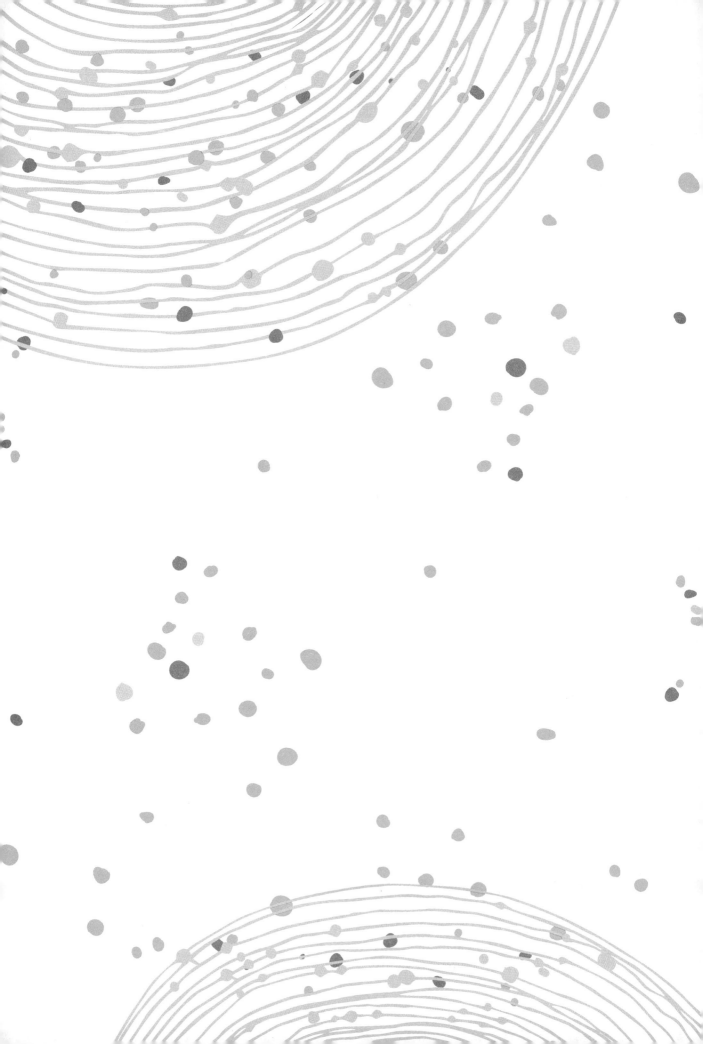

Choice Reading Project (A)

Spelling List 17 Pretest

1. Open the Spelling Pretest activity online. Listen to the first spelling word. Type the word. Check your answer.

2. Write the correct spelling of the word in the Word column of the Spelling Pretest table on the next page.

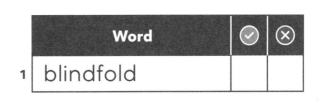

Word	✓	✗
1 blindfold		

3. Put a check mark in the ✓ column if you spelled the word correctly online.

Word	✓	✗
1 blindfold	✓	

Put an X in the ✗ column if you spelled the word incorrectly online.

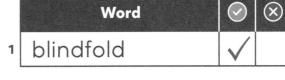

Word	✓	✗
1 blindfold		✗

4. Repeat Steps 1–3 for the remaining words in the Spelling Pretest.

Choice Reading Project (A)

Spelling List 17 Pretest

Write each spelling word in the Word column, making sure to spell it correctly.

	Word	✓	✕
1			
2			
3			
4			
5			
6			
7			
8			
9			
10			
11			

	Word	✓	✕
12			
13			
14			
15			
16			
17			
18			
19			
20			
21			

Choice Reading Project (B)

Spelling List 17 Activity Bank

Circle any words in the box that you did not spell correctly on the pretest. Using your circled words, complete one activity of your choice. Complete as much of the activity as you can in the time given.

If you spelled all words correctly on the pretest, complete your chosen activity with as many spelling words as you can.

absence	recent	twice	script	acceptable
ancestor	rejoice	description	transcript	honorable
citizen	scene	manuscript	Indiana	predictable
conceited	science	prescription	Missouri	respectable
fragrance				

Spelling Activity Choices

Vowel-Free Words

1. In the left column, write only the consonants in each word and put a dot where each vowel should be.

2. Spell each word out loud, stating which vowels should be in the places you wrote dots.

3. In the right column, rewrite the entire spelling word.

4. Correct any spelling errors.

Alphabetizing

1. In the left column, write your words from the spelling word list in alphabetical order.

2. Correct any spelling errors.

Parts of Speech

1. In the left column, write the words from your spelling list that are nouns.

2. In the right column, write all the other words from your spelling list and label each word's part of speech.

3. Correct any spelling errors.

Uppercase and Lowercase

1. In the left column, write each of your words in all capital (uppercase) letters.

2. In the right column, write each of your words in all lowercase letters.

3. Correct any spelling errors.

Complete the activity that you chose.

My chosen activity: _____

1. _____   _____
2. _____   _____
3. _____   _____
4. _____   _____
5. _____   _____
6. _____   _____
7. _____   _____
8. _____   _____
9. _____   _____
10. _____   _____
11. _____   _____
12. _____   _____
13. _____   _____
14. _____   _____
15. _____   _____
16. _____   _____
17. _____   _____
18. _____   _____
19. _____   _____
20. _____   _____
21. _____   _____
22. _____   _____
23. _____   _____
24. _____   _____
25. _____   _____

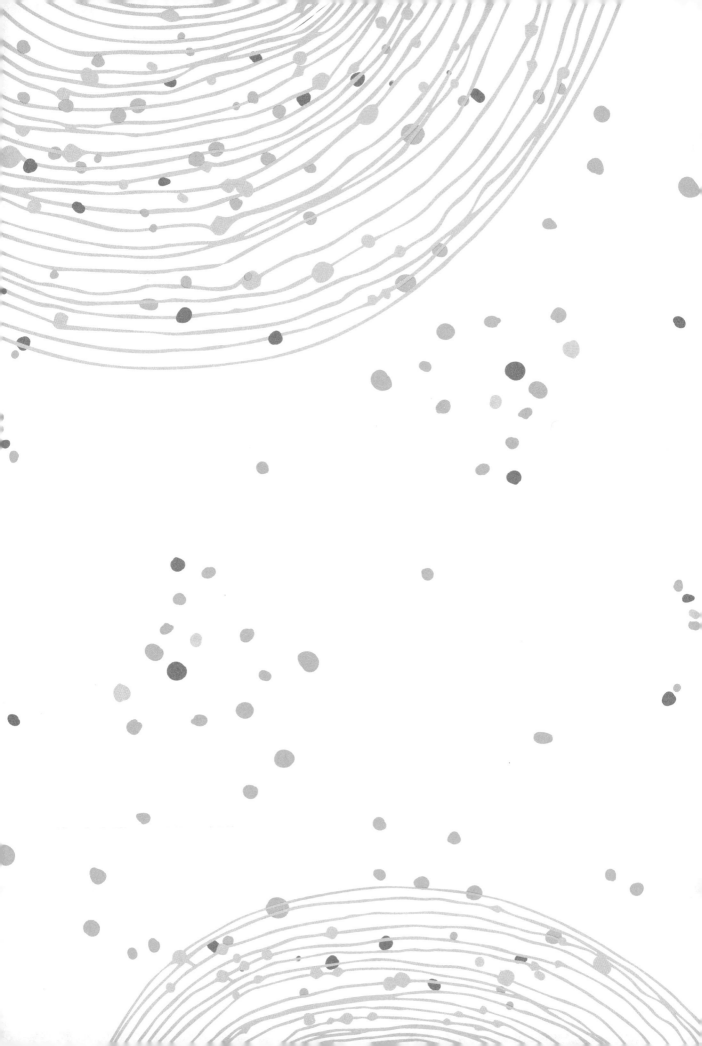

Choice Reading Project (F)

Spelling List 18 Pretest

1. Open the Spelling Pretest activity online. Listen to the first spelling word. Type the word. Check your answer.

2. Write the correct spelling of the word in the Word column of the Spelling Pretest table on the next page.

Word	✓	✗
1 blindfold		

3. Put a check mark in the ✓ column if you spelled the word correctly online.

Word	✓	✗
1 blindfold	✓	

Put an X in the ✗ column if you spelled the word incorrectly online.

Word	✓	✗
1 blindfold		X

4. Repeat Steps 1–3 for the remaining words in the Spelling Pretest.

Choice Reading Project (F)

Spelling List 18 Pretest

Write each spelling word in the Word column, making sure to spell it correctly.

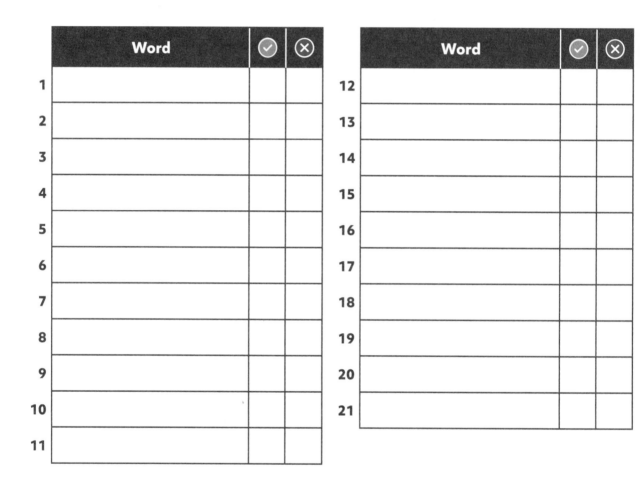

	Word	✓	✗
1			
2			
3			
4			
5			
6			
7			
8			
9			
10			
11			

	Word	✓	✗
12			
13			
14			
15			
16			
17			
18			
19			
20			
21			

Choice Reading Project (G)

Spelling List 18 Activity Bank

Circle any words in the box that you did not spell correctly on the pretest. Using your circled words, complete one activity of your choice. Complete as much of the activity as you can in the time given.

If you spelled all words correctly on the pretest, complete your chosen activity with as many spelling words as you can.

announcement	probing	tasteful	capture	humiliation
balanced	relieved	capsule	capacity	location
immediately	sharing	captivate	North Carolina	occupation
likely	sincerely	captive	West Virginia	starvation
motivated				

Spelling Activity Choices

Hidden Words

1. Draw a picture and "hide" as many words from the Spelling Word List as they can inside the picture.

2. See if others can find the words within the picture.

Triangle Spelling

Write each word in a triangle.

Ghost Words

1. Use a white crayon to write each spelling word.

2. Go over the white crayon writing with a colored marker.

Complete the activity that you chose.

My chosen activity: _____

Apply: Latin Affixes

Rewrite the sentences or add a second sentence to give a context clue for each vocabulary word's meaning. The first one has been done for you.

1. I went to hear a **famous** author speak.

   New sentence: I went to hear a **famous** author speak. He is well-known because many of his books have been made into movies.

2. It was **disastrous** when Rico's dad lost his wallet.

   _____

   _____

   _____

   _____

   _____

3. My friend always feels **anxious** when she rides her bike.

   _____

   _____

   _____

   _____

   _____

Answer the questions. Use the vocabulary word in your response and be sure to include enough context so a reader could determine the meaning of the word. Use complete sentences in your responses.

4. What is something that would seem like **nonsense** to you?

_____

_____

_____

_____

_____

_____

5. Imagine a fiction book about a mummy and a **nonfiction** book about a mummy. How might these books be different?

_____

_____

_____

_____

_____

_____

Opinion Writing: Prewriting (A)

Spelling List 19 Pretest

1. Open the Spelling Pretest activity online. Listen to the first spelling word. Type the word. Check your answer.

2. Write the correct spelling of the word in the Word column of the Spelling Pretest table on the next page.

Word	✓	✗
1 blindfold		

3. Put a check mark in the ✓ column if you spelled the word correctly online.

Word	✓	✗
1 blindfold	✓	

Put an X in the ✗ column if you spelled the word incorrectly online.

Word	✓	✗
1 blindfold		X

4. Repeat Steps 1–3 for the remaining words in the Spelling Pretest.

Opinion Writing: Prewriting (A)

Spelling List 19 Pretest

Write each spelling word in the Word column, making sure to spell it correctly.

	Word	✓	✕
1			
2			
3			
4			
5			
6			
7			
8			
9			
10			
11			

	Word	✓	✕
12			
13			
14			
15			
16			
17			
18			
19			
20			
21			

Opinion Writing: Prewriting (A)

Brainstorm for Your Opinion Essay

Read the writing assignment. You will complete the assignment in steps over multiple lessons.

Prompt: **Write an opinion essay on a topic of your choice.**

Requirements: Your essay should include the following:

- A **title**

- An **introduction** that introduces the topic, includes your opinion, and provides an organizational structure

- **Three body paragraphs**, each centered on a reason for your opinion with important facts and details that support your opinion

- **Transitions** that link your opinion and reasons, and your reasons and evidence

- At least one **personal experience** related to the topic

- Information discovered during **research**

- A **conclusion** that restates your opinion in different words and wraps up the text

- Correct **grammar**, **usage**, and **mechanics**

- A list of at least **two trustworthy sources**, one of which is a print source, such as a newspaper, magazine, book, or encyclopedia. The other source may be a digital source found on the Internet, such as a government website.

Audience: Your teacher and peers

Purpose: Explain your opinion about a topic to readers.

Length: 350 to 500 words long (1 to 2 typed, double-spaced pages)

Brainstorm and choose a topic for your opinion essay.

1. Think about topics important to you, and list your opinions on those topics. List as many of your opinions as you can. Use the sentence starters to help you.

My opinion is:

I think:

I believe:

I feel:

2. Read your opinions. Cross out any that
   - Don't really interest you
   - Seem too large or broad

3. Circle the opinions that you would like to write about. If you didn't circle any opinions, add a few more.

4. Choose your favorite opinion among those that you circled. Then answer Yes or No to each of the following questions:

    a. Is the topic this opinion represents focused enough to cover in detail in five paragraphs? _____

    b. Is the topic something you can research using trustworthy sources?

    _____

    c. Is the topic interesting to you? _____

5. Did you answer Yes to Parts A–C of Question 4? You have found your opinion topic! If not, go back to another opinion that you circled and go through the questions for that topic. Repeat until you find one that works.

The opinion topic for my essay is

_____

_____

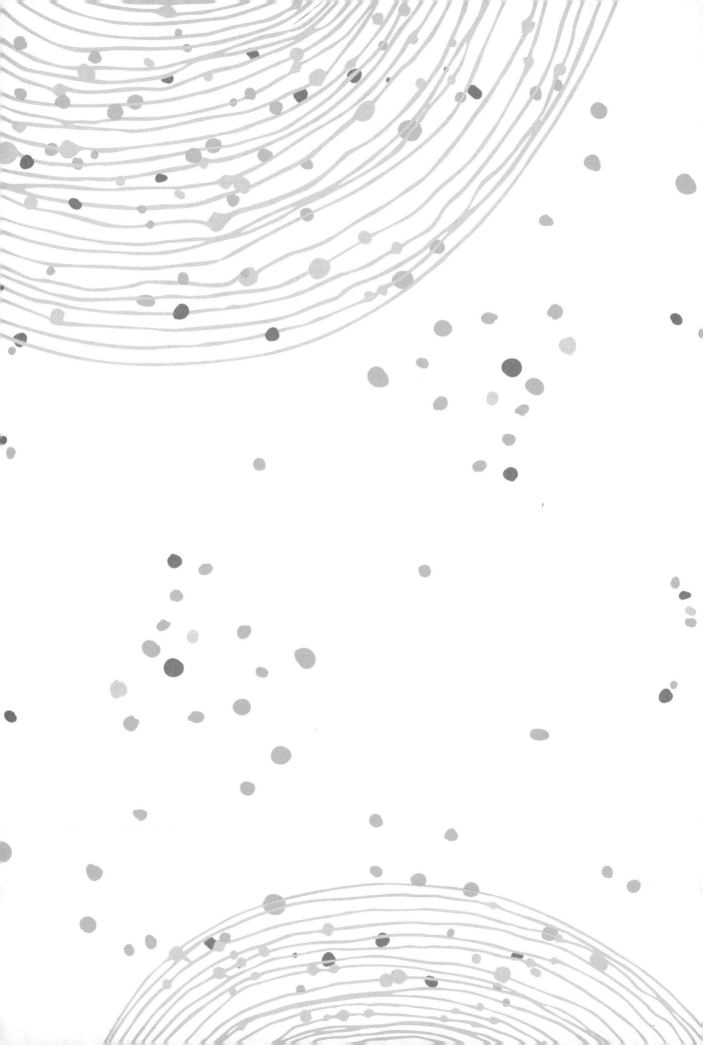

Opinion Writing: Prewriting (B)

Spelling List 19 Activity Bank

Circle any words in the box that you did not spell correctly on the pretest. Using your circled words, complete one activity of your choice. Complete as much of the activity as you can in the time given.

If you spelled all words correctly on the pretest, complete your chosen activity with as many spelling words as you can.

betrayed	relaying	worrying	incredible	journalist
cozier	supplying	credible	California	scientist
displaying	surveyed	credit	Minnesota	violinist
heaviest	angrier	discredit	dentist	nutritionist
laziest				

Spelling Activity Choices

Create a Crossword

1. Write a word from your spelling word list in the center of the grid paper.

2. Write another spelling word going across and sharing a letter with the first word. See how many words you can connect.

   Example:

				p			
			k	i	s	s	e	s
		d		n			
	r	o	c	k	s		
		g					
		s					

Word Search Puzzle

1. Draw a box on the grid paper. The box should be large enough to hold your words from the spelling word list.

2. Fill in the grid paper with words from your spelling list, writing them horizontally, vertically, and diagonally (forward and backward if you choose).

3. Fill in the rest of the box with random letters.

4. Ask someone to find and circle your spelling words in the puzzle you made.

Complete the activity that you chose.

My chosen activity: _____

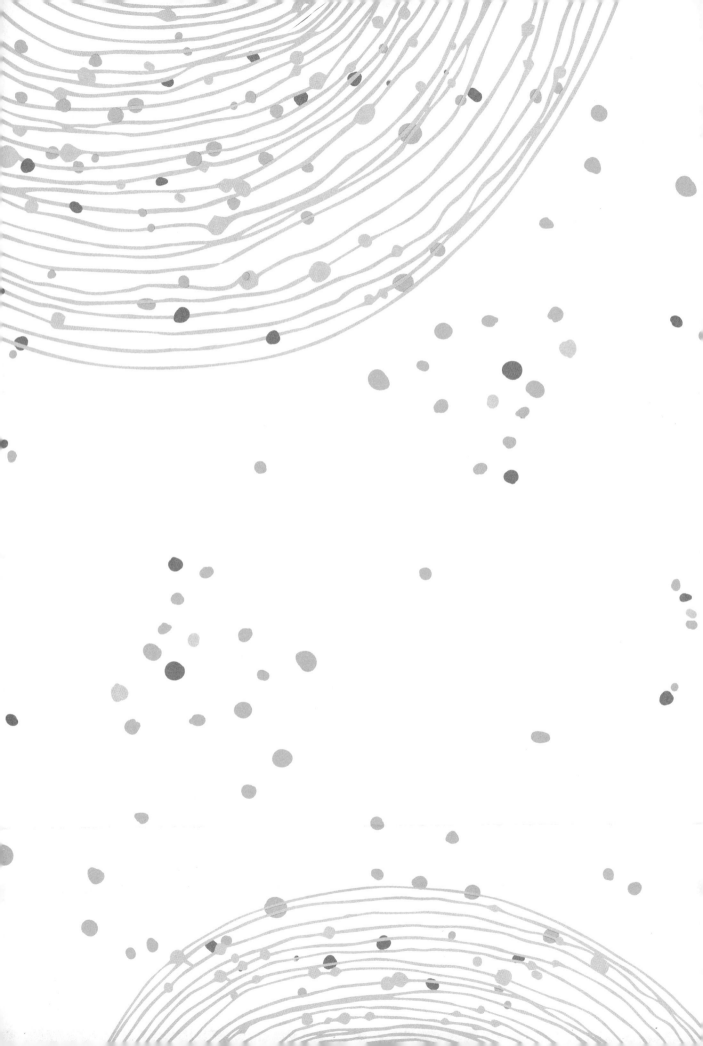

Opinion Writing: Prewriting (B)

Conduct Research for Your Opinion Essay

Follow these steps to write a research question.

1. Write the opinion that you are supporting in your opinion essay.

   Sample opinion:

   I think that cats make an ideal pet.

   Opinion:

   _____

   _____

2. Write a question that you can research to support your opinion.

   Sample research question:

   What traits do cats possess that make them good pets?

   Research question:

   _____

   _____

Follow these steps to conduct research. Record information on the Research Notes pages that follow. Use one page per source.

3. Identify at least two sources. Record the title, author, publisher, and URL of each source.

   - One source must be a print source, such as a book, an article originally published in a newspaper or magazine, a pamphlet, or an encyclopedia article.

   - One source must be a digital source found on the Internet.

4. As you read each source, take notes about information related to your research question.

   - Write your notes in your own words.

   - If you find a direct quotation that you think you might use in your essay, record the quotation, word for word, in quotation marks. Also record the name of the person you are quoting.

I'm searching for facts about how much cats love laundry baskets.

Research Notes

Source

Title: _____

Author: _____

Published by: _____

URL (if necessary): _____

Notes

Key Information Written in Your Own Words:

_____

_____

_____

_____

_____

_____

_____

Direct Quotation:

_____

_____

_____

Person Quoted: _____

Research Notes

Source

Title: _____

Author: _____

Published by: _____

URL (if necessary): _____

Notes

Key Information Written in Your Own Words:

_____

_____

_____

_____

_____

_____

Direct Quotation:

_____

_____

_____

Person Quoted: _____

Opinion Writing: Prewriting (C)

Prewrite Your Opinion Essay

Use your research notes to complete the O.R.E.O. graphic organizer for your opinion essay. You do not need to answer in complete sentences.

Note: Write at least one personal experience in one of the "Evidence" sections of your graphic organizer.

Opinion:

_____

_____

Reason 1: _____

Evidence: _____

_____

_____

Reason 2: _____

Evidence: _____

_____

_____

Reason 3: _____

Evidence: _____

_____

_____

Opinion, reworded:

_____

_____

Opinion Writing: Drafting (A)

Draft Your Opinion Essay

Using your notes and your graphic organizer to guide you, write the
first draft of your opinion essay. Write only on the white rows. You
will use the purple rows for revisions later.

Title _____

start here ▶

keep writing ▶

Draft Page 1

keep writing ▶

Draft Page 2

keep writing ▶

Draft Page 3

Draft Page 4

Pink and Say

Spelling List 20 Pretest

1. Open the Spelling Pretest activity online. Listen to the first spelling word. Type the word. Check your answer.

2. Write the correct spelling of the word in the Word column of the Spelling Pretest table on the next page.

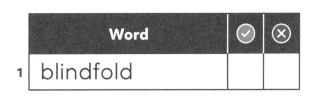

	Word	✓	✕
1	blindfold		

3. Put a check mark in the ✓ column if you spelled the word correctly online.

	Word	✓	✕
1	blindfold	✓	

Put an X in the ✕ column if you spelled the word incorrectly online.

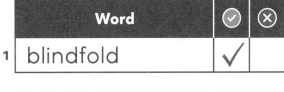

	Word	✓	✕
1	blindfold		✕

4. Repeat Steps 1–3 for the remaining words in the Spelling Pretest.

Pink and Say

Spelling List 20 Pretest

Write each spelling word in the Word column, making sure to spell it correctly.

	Word	✓	✕
1			
2			
3			
4			
5			
6			
7			
8			
9			
10			
11			
12			
13			

	Word	✓	✕
14			
15			
16			
17			
18			
19			
20			
21			
22			
23			
24			
25			

Write from Another Character's Perspective

Read the passage from *Pink and Say* by Patricia Polacco.

Think about how *Pink and Say* would be different if the story were told from Moe Moe Bay's perspective. Rewrite the following section of the text from Moe Moe Bay's perspective. Write your response in complete sentences.

Then fever must have took me good, 'cause I could feel a cool, sweet-smelling quilt next to my face. Soft, gentle warm hands were strokin' my head with a cool wet rag cloth.

"Look at that mornin' that's comin'," a woman's voice said as she spooned oat porridge into me. "Do your momma know what a beautiful baby boy she has?"

"Where am I? Is this heaven?" I asked.

She tossed her head and laughed. "No child, Pinkus brung you home to me—don't you remember?"

The mahogany child, I thought.

"Both you children been on the run for days, and a miracle of God Almighty brung you both here, yes indeed, child, a miracle."

Pink and Say Wrap-Up

Spelling List 20 Activity Bank

Circle any words in the box that you did not spell correctly on the pretest. Using your circled words, complete one activity of your choice. Complete as much of the activity as you can in the time given.

If you spelled all words correctly on the pretest, complete your chosen activity with as many spelling words as you can.

counties	journeys	activities	sensational	collector
diaries	kidneys	daisies	sensible	counselor
highways	libraries	birthdays	sensitive	director
hobbies	territories	supplies	Massachusetts	governor
holidays	valleys	nonsense	Washington	senator

Spelling Activity Choices

Vowel-Free Words

1. In the left column, write only the consonants in each word and put a dot where each vowel should be.

2. Spell each word out loud, stating which vowels should be in the places you wrote dots.

3. In the right column, rewrite the entire spelling word.

4. Correct any spelling errors.

Alphabetizing

1. In the left column, write your words from the spelling word list in alphabetical order.

2. Correct any spelling errors.

Parts of Speech

1. In the left column, write the words from your spelling list that are nouns.

2. In the right column, write all the other words from your spelling list and label each word's part of speech.

3. Correct any spelling errors.

Uppercase and Lowercase

1. In the left column, write each of your words in all capital letters, or all uppercase.

2. In the right column, write each of your words in all lowercase letters.

3. Correct any spelling errors.

Complete the activity that you chose.

My chosen activity: _____

1. _____   _____
2. _____   _____
3. _____   _____
4. _____   _____
5. _____   _____
6. _____   _____
7. _____   _____
8. _____   _____
9. _____   _____
10. _____   _____
11. _____   _____
12. _____   _____
13. _____   _____
14. _____   _____
15. _____   _____
16. _____   _____
17. _____   _____
18. _____   _____
19. _____   _____
20. _____   _____
21. _____   _____
22. _____   _____
23. _____   _____
24. _____   _____
25. _____   _____

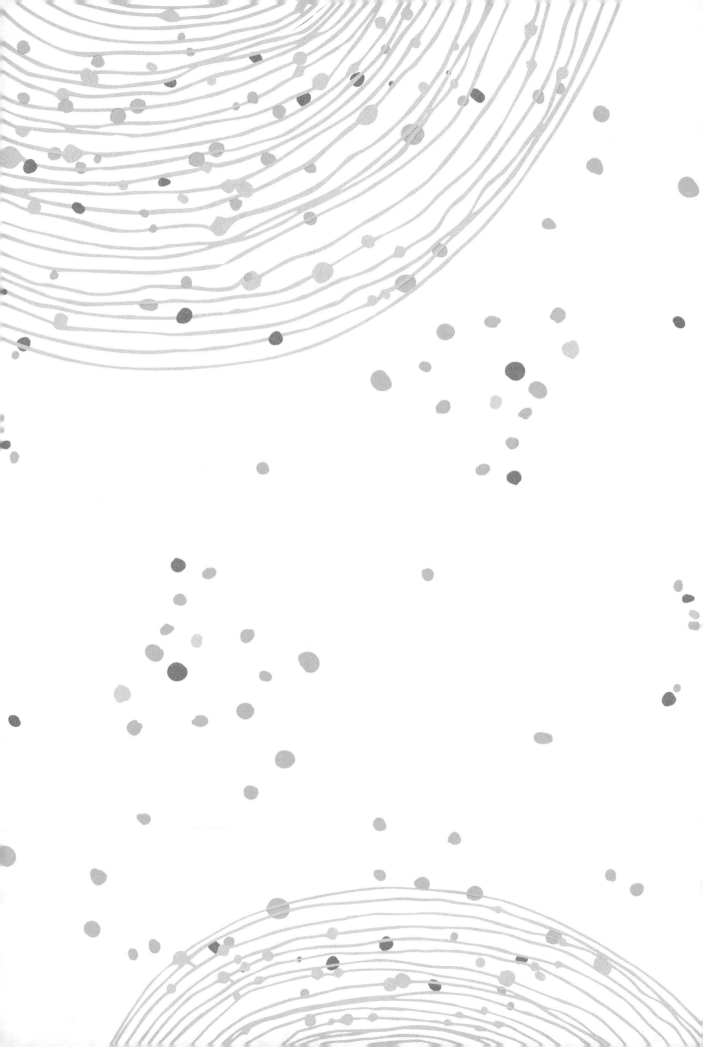

Pink and Say Wrap-Up

Write About the Author's Perspective in *Pink and Say*

Write your responses in complete sentences.

1. What is the author's purpose for writing *Pink and Say*?

_____

_____

_____

_____

_____

_____

_____

2. Do you think that Patricia Polacco achieved her purpose? Be sure to explain your reasoning in 1 or 2 sentences.

_____

_____

_____

_____

_____

_____

3. Why do you think the author wrote the story from Sheldon's perspective and not Pinkus's?

_____

_____

_____

_____

_____

_____

4. Why do you think the author included a note at the end of the story?

_____

_____

_____

_____

_____

_____

5. What do you think Polacco's attitude is toward what happened to Pinkus? Use details from the author's note to support your reasoning.

_____

_____

_____

_____

_____

"Ibrahim"

Write About Inferences and Conclusions

Write your responses in complete sentences.

1. At the end of the story, Ibrahim is reunited with his mother. This passage from the story describes her reaction: "She smiled and she thanked God. She kissed him and kissed him and kissed him."

   What inferences can you make about how Ibrahim's mother feels when she is reunited with Ibrahim? Explain how the sentences from the story support your inferences.

_____

_____

_____

_____

_____

_____

_____

_____

_____

_____

_____

_____

2. What conclusion can you draw about how Ibrahim's mother felt when Ibrahim was lost? What inferences or details in the text support your conclusion?

_____

_____

_____

_____

_____

_____

_____

_____

_____

_____

_____

_____

3. What conclusion can you draw about what Ibrahim's mother may have been doing while Ibrahim was missing? What inferences or details in the text support your conclusion?

_____

_____

_____

_____

_____

_____

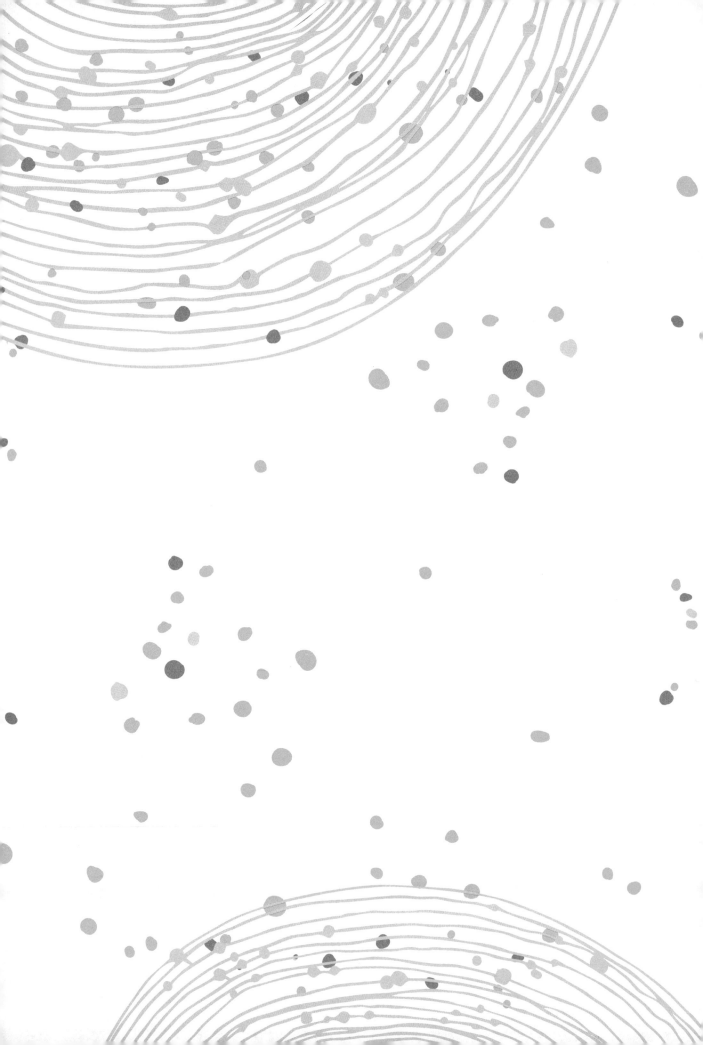

"Ibrahim" Wrap-Up

Write About Theme in "Ibrahim"

Write your responses in complete sentences.

1. What is Ibrahim's problem in the story?

   _____

   _____

2. What are some of the ways that Mary helps Ibrahim?

   _____

   _____

   _____

   _____

   _____

   _____

   _____

3. Who are some of the other people that help Ibrahim, and how do they help him?

   _____

   _____

   _____

   _____

   _____

   _____

_____

_____

_____

_____

_____

_____

_____

_____

_____

_____

_____

_____

_____

4. Based on your answers to Questions 1–3, what is one of the themes of "Ibrahim"? Circle your choice.

Most people are able to solve problems on their own.

When people work together they can solve problems.

Baseball Saved Us

How Do Cause and Effect Affect Character?

Write your responses in complete sentences.

1. The challenges that characters face in a story are the causes of many events in the plot.

   What are some challenges that the main character (Shorty) faces throughout the story?

_____

_____

_____

_____

_____

_____

_____

_____

_____

_____

2. The effects of these causes, or challenges, are what the characters do to overcome them.

What steps does Shorty take to overcome those challenges?

_____

_____

_____

_____

_____

_____

_____

_____

_____

_____

_____

3. What do the relationships between cause and effect in the story reveal about Shorty's character?

_____

_____

_____

_____

My hand is starting to feel numb. What could possibly be the cause?

Baseball Saved Us Wrap-Up

Write About Theme in *Baseball Saved Us*

Write your responses in complete sentences.

1. What is one of the themes in the book *Baseball Saved Us*? Write a paragraph explaining the theme.

_____

_____

_____

_____

_____

_____

_____

2. What details from the story support the theme you identified in Question 1?

_____

_____

_____

_____

_____

_____

_____

_____

_____

_____

_____

_____

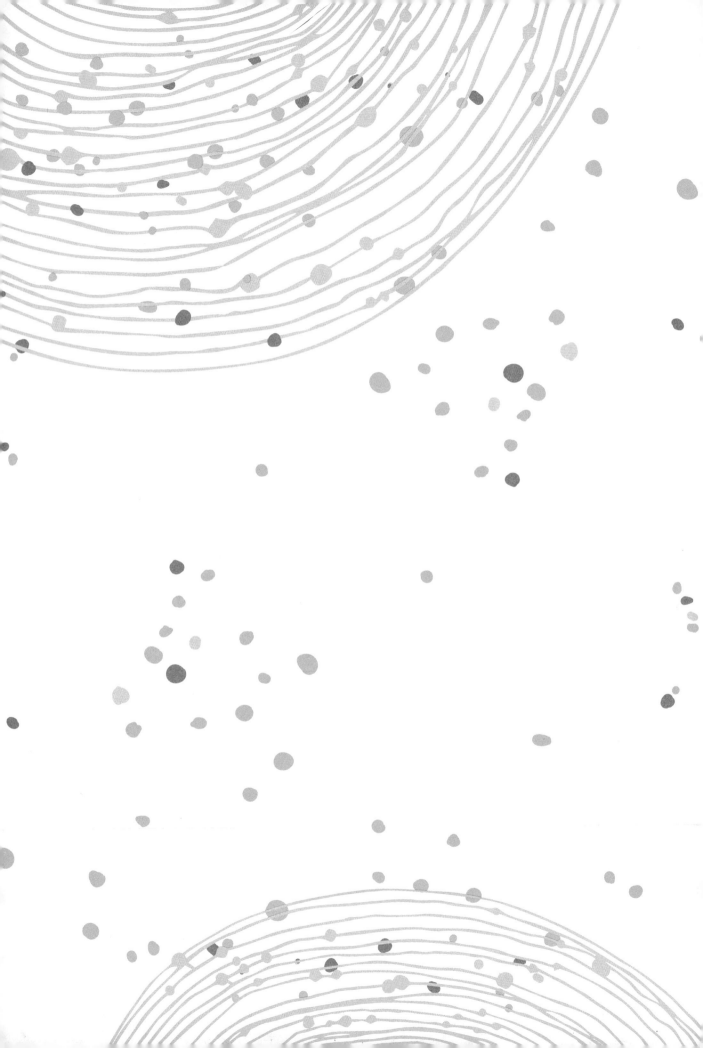

Opinion Writing: Revising

Revise Your Opinion Essay

Use the checklist as you revise your opinion essay draft.

Organization

☐ Does my essay have an introduction, at least three body paragraphs, and a conclusion?

☐ Does each paragraph begin with a topic sentence?

☐ Are supporting facts and details grouped in the correct body paragraphs?

☐ Do I use clear and logical transitions?

Content

☐ Does my introduction clearly state the topic and my opinion?

☐ Does each body paragraph focus on a reason that supports my opinion?

☐ Do I use enough facts and details, including at least one personal experience, to support each reason?

☐ Is my essay factual and well researched?

☐ Are the words I use precise and domain-specific?

☐ Does my conclusion restate my opinion and reasons, using different words?

☐ Do I have a source list that includes at least two research sources, one print and one digital?

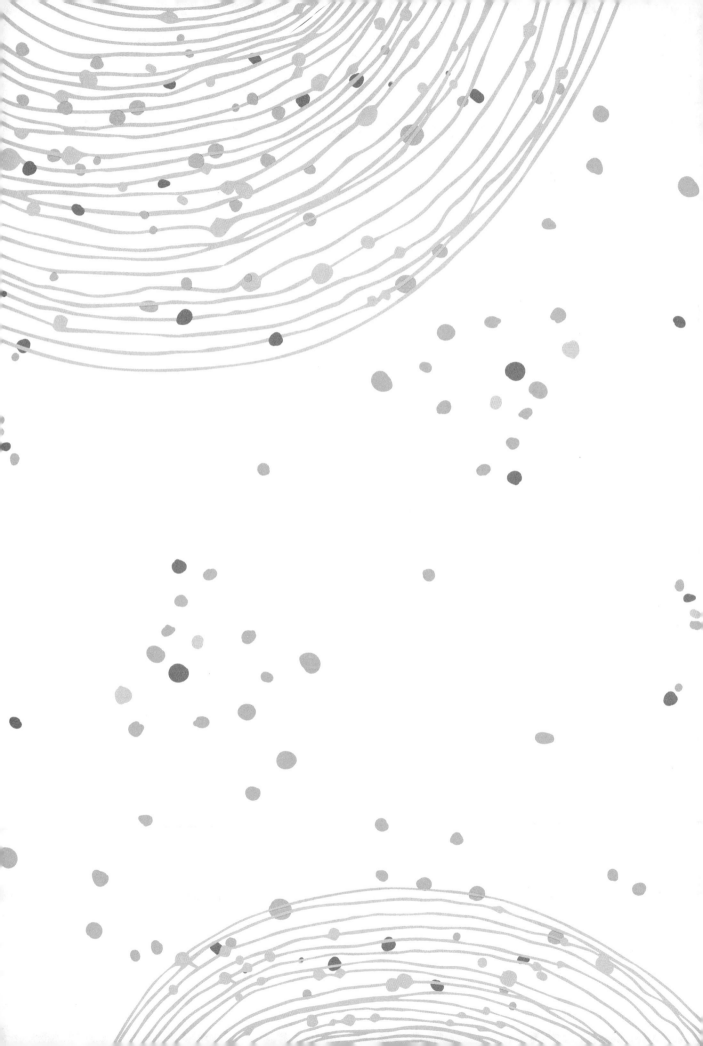

Opinion Writing: Proofreading

Proofread Your Opinion Essay

Use the checklist as you proofread your revised opinion essay draft.

Grammar and Usage

☐ Are all sentences complete and correct?

☐ Are there any missing or extra words?

☐ Are helping verbs used correctly, such as using can vs. could to express a particular meaning?

☐ Are prepositional phrases used to add information to sentences?

☐ Are relative pronouns and relative adverbs used correctly?

☐ Are there other grammatical or usage errors?

Mechanics

☐ Is every word spelled correctly, including frequently confused words?

☐ Does every sentence begin with a capital letter and end with the appropriate punctuation?

☐ Is punctuation used thoughtfully and effectively?

☐ Are the titles of works in the source list capitalized correctly?

☐ Are there other punctuation or capitalization errors?

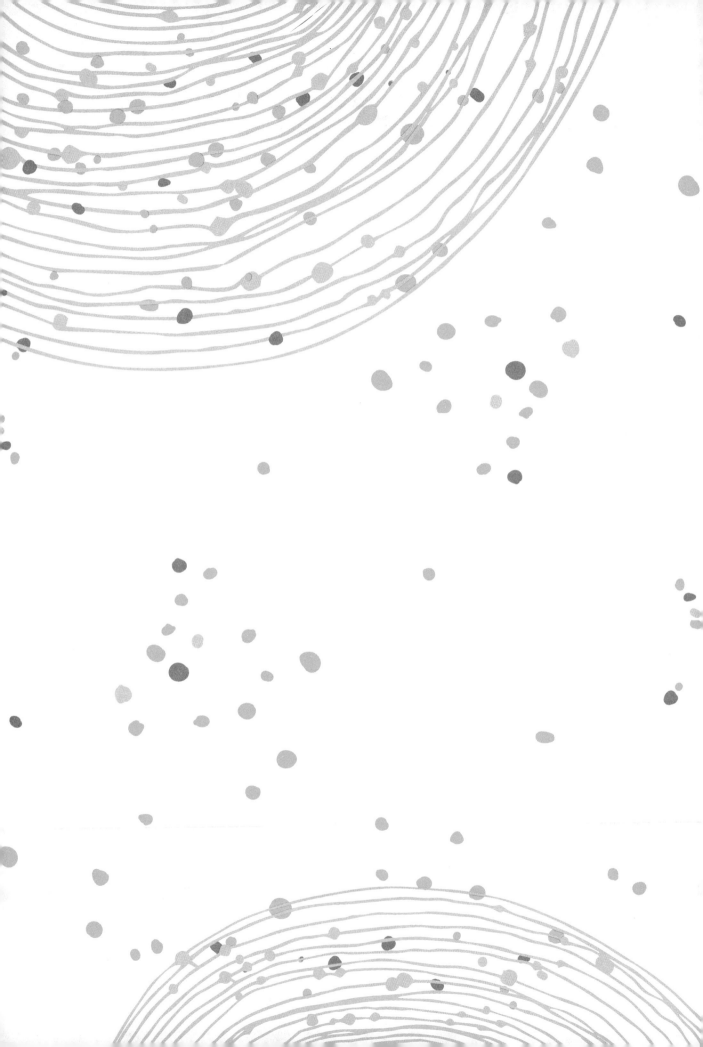

Apply: Greek Roots

Answer the questions. Use complete sentences in your responses to questions that ask for an explanation.

1. The word *hydrate* means "to give water to or to drink water." Which word means the opposite of *hydrate*—*hydrant* or *dehydrate*? Explain why that word is the opposite of *hydrate*.

_____

_____

_____

_____

_____

_____

2. The prefix *re-* means "again." What word could you form that means "to give water to again"?

_____

_____

3. Why might you need to rehydrate a plant? Explain how you would do it. Be sure to use the word *rehydrate* in your answer.

_____

_____

_____

_____

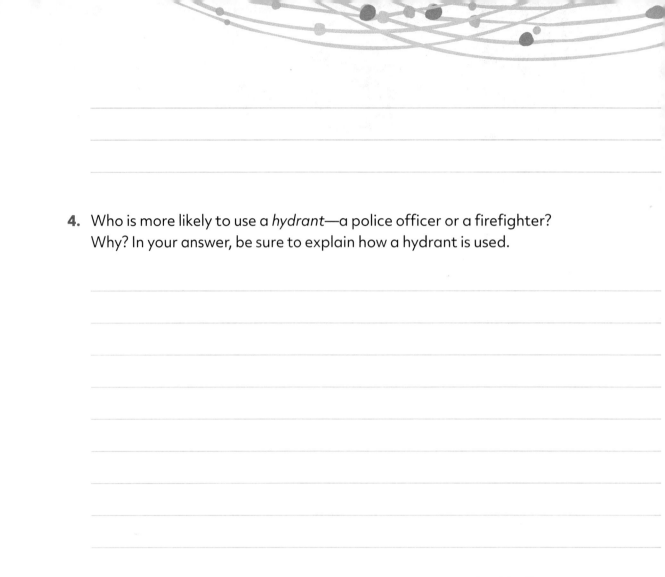

4. Who is more likely to use a *hydrant*—a police officer or a firefighter? Why? In your answer, be sure to explain how a hydrant is used.

5. The definition of *dermatology* is "the science of or the study of the skin." The definition of *biology* is "the science of or the study of life." What word means the "the science or study of water"?

6. List two additional words that contain the Greek root *hydro*. You may want to refer to a dictionary.

"Maria Gonzalez, Modern Hero"

Spelling List 21 Pretest

1. Open the Spelling Pretest activity online. Listen to the first spelling word. Type the word. Check your answer.

2. Write the correct spelling of the word in the Word column of the Spelling Pretest table on the next page.

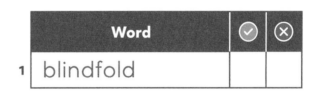

3. Put a check mark in the ✓ column if you spelled the word correctly online.

   Put an X in the ✗ column if you spelled the word incorrectly online.

4. Repeat Steps 1–3 for the remaining words in the Spelling Pretest.

"Maria Gonzalez, Modern Hero"

Spelling List 21 Pretest

Write each spelling word in the Word column, making sure to spell it correctly.

	Word	✓	✗
1			
2			
3			
4			
5			
6			
7			
8			
9			

	Word	✓	✗
10			
11			
12			
13			
14			
15			
16			
17			

"Maria Gonzalez, Modern Hero"

A Herculean Task

A Herculean task refers to the Greek hero Hercules. Hercules is known for his great strength and the effort he put forth to complete 12 tasks that seemed impossible. These tasks included defeating a lion with skin like armor and a nine-headed snake. So a Herculean task would be a task that seems impossible and would take a great deal of strength and effort to complete.

1. Which of the following would be considered a Herculean task? Circle the answer.

    a. Changing the path of a river

    b. Painting a house

    c. Walking three dogs

2. What is something you believe would be a Herculean task for a fourth grader? Write a paragraph describing the task and how you would complete it. Use complete sentences in your response.

_____

_____

_____

_____

_____

_____

_____

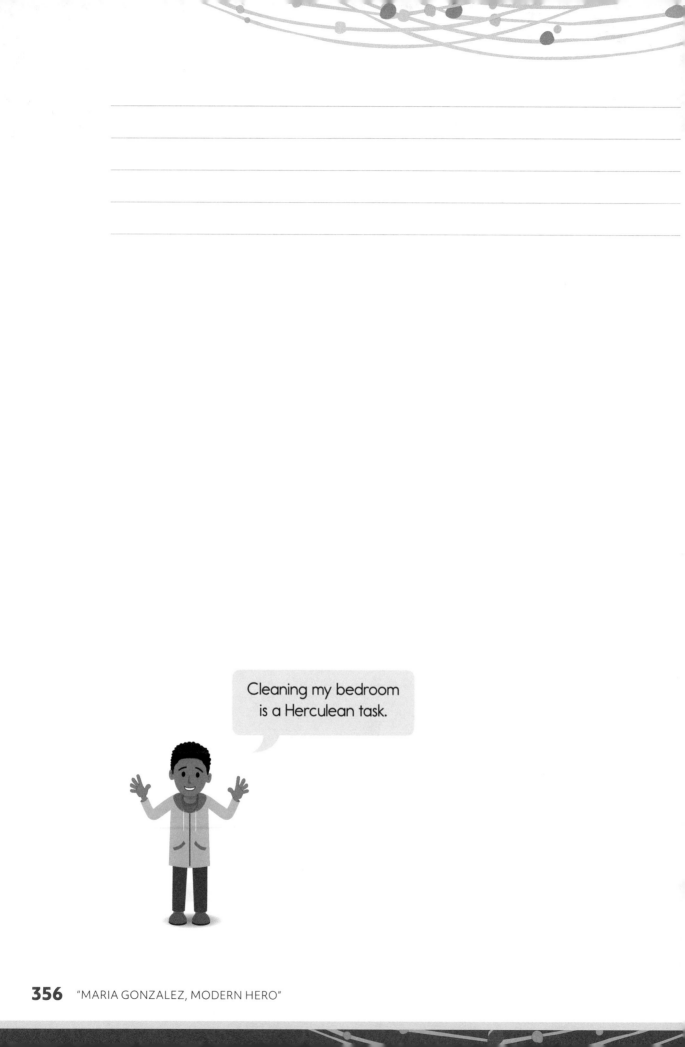

Cleaning my bedroom
is a Herculean task.

"Maria Gonzalez, Modern Hero" Wrap-Up

Spelling List 21 Activity Bank

Circle any words in the box that you did not spell correctly on the pretest. Using your circled words, complete one activity of your choice. Complete as much of the activity as you can in the time given.

If you spelled all words correctly on the pretest, complete your chosen activity with as many spelling words as you can.

dolphin	trophy	guide	audible	audition
hyphen	guard	guilty	audience	Idaho
philosophy	guess	guitar	audio	South Dakota
photograph	guest			

Spelling Activity Choices

Silly Sentences

1. Write a silly sentence using your words from the spelling word list.

2. Underline the spelling word in each sentence.
   Example: The dog was <u>driving</u> a car.

3. Correct any spelling errors.

Spelling Story

1. Write a very short story using your words from the spelling word list.

2. Underline the spelling words in the story.

3. Correct any spelling errors.

Riddle Me This

1. Write a riddle for your words from the spelling word list.
   Example: "I have a trunk, but it's not on my car."

2. Write the answer, which is your word, for each riddle.
   Example: Answer: elephant

3. Correct any spelling errors.

RunOnWord

1. Gather some crayons, colored pencils, or markers. Write each of your words, using a different color for each word, end to end as one long word.
   Example: dogcatbirdfishturtle

2. Rewrite the words correctly and with proper spacing.

Complete the activity that you chose.

My chosen activity: _____

_____

_____

_____

_____

_____

_____

_____

_____

_____

_____

_____

_____

_____

_____

_____

_____

_____

_____

_____

_____

_____

_____

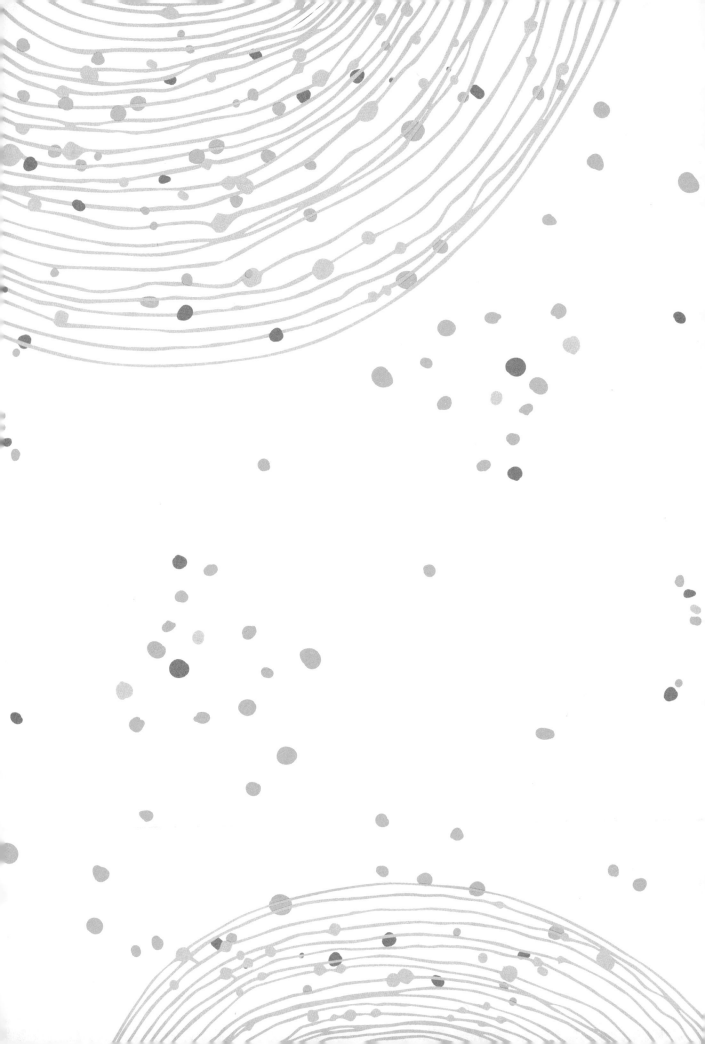

"Maria Gonzalez, Modern Hero" Wrap-Up

Match Them Up

Read the descriptions of characters from mythology. Then match each character to the person that has the same traits. Explain why the person described matches the character from mythology.

Character	Description
Echo	Echo offended the goddess Hera. Hera took away Echo's gift of speech and cursed her to only repeat the last words of others.
Narcissus	Narcissus was very beautiful. He fell in love with his own reflection in a pool of water. He stared at his own image for so long that he forgot to eat and drink, until he wasted away and died.
Sisyphus	Sisyphus was a clever king who fooled the gods. He was punished by Hades in the underworld by having to push a boulder up a steep hill. Every time he had almost reached the top, the boulder rolled to the bottom, and he had to start over again.
Pandora	The god Zeus made Pandora extremely curious. Then he gave her a sealed jar and told her that she must never open it. Pandora could not control her curiosity. She opened the jar and released all the evils that make people miserable, such as greed, lies, and envy.

1. Magda is so vain that she cannot pass by a mirror without stopping to look at herself.

   Which mythological character is Magda like and why?

   _____

   _____

   _____

2. Jojo never has any ideas of his own. He just copies others and repeats what they say.

   Which mythological character is Jojo like and why?

   _____

   _____

   _____

3. I don't like being around Hannah. It seems like she always causes trouble and makes people miserable.

   Which mythological character is Hannah like and why?

   _____

   _____

   _____

Read the description of Sisyphus and complete the following task. Use complete sentences in your response.

4. Write a description of a person who is similar to Sisyphus.

   _____

   _____

   _____

"Grace"

Write a Summary of "Grace"

Write your responses in complete sentences.

Write a summary of "Grace." Be sure to include the most important characters and events from the beginning, middle, and end of the story. Also include any important ideas, such as a lesson Grace may have learned.

_____

_____

_____

_____

_____

_____

_____

_____

_____

_____

_____

_____

_____

_____

_____

_____

"Grace" Wrap-Up

Write About Theme in "Grace"

Write your responses in complete sentences.

What is a theme the author conveys in "Grace"? Write a paragraph
explaining the theme. Be sure to include examples of how the actions of the
story's characters support the theme.

_____

_____

_____

_____

_____

_____

_____

_____

_____

_____

_____

_____

_____

_____

_____

_____

Presentation Skills (A)

Tell About an Experience

Use the prompt to answer the questions.

Prompt: **Give an informal speech and a formal speech about an experience you had. Each speech should be about one minute long.**

1. Write notes about what you will say in the beginning, middle, and end of your speech. Then list any words or phrases you will say differently when you speak informally and formally. Some sample notes are shown.

Sequence of Events	Notes for Informal Speech	Notes for Formal Speech
Beginning – Watching a movie with Jacob at his house – Didn't know we would be part of the action	saw a movie at Jake's	viewed a motion picture at the Cohen residence

Sequence of Events	Notes for Informal Speech	Notes for Formal Speech
Middle		
End		

2. Deliver your speeches to your Learning Coach.

3. How were your two speeches different?

_____

_____

_____

Read Aloud Like a Pro

1. Record yourself reading the following excerpt from "Cinderella."

Once upon a time, in a country village, there lived a lovely young maiden. This maiden was gentle and kindhearted. She had lived a happy and comfortable life with her loving mother and father in their own grand estate until the untimely death of her mother. Her father soon looked for a new woman to marry so that his daughter would once again have a mother.

The maiden's father met a widow who was raising two daughters of her own. Her daughters were similar in age to his daughter. The widow and her daughters seemed kind, so the two quickly married. Then the woman and her two daughters moved in. Sadly, the new mother and her daughters were actually not kind. They pretended to be nice whenever the father was around. But when his daughter was left alone with her new family members, they treated her poorly. They made her do all the chores and wait on them like a servant.

"Do the mending!" yelled her stepmother.

"Sweep the steps!" yelled her stepsister.

"Where is our food!?!" yelled her other stepsister.

2. Listen to what you recorded.

   a. Did you speak too quickly or too slowly during any parts of your speech? Identify one way you could improve your pace.

   _____

   _____

   b. Did you speak all words clearly? Identify one way you could improve your clarity.

   _____

   _____

3. Record yourself reading the passage again. Use your answers to Question 2 to improve your pace and clarity.

I never realized how fast I spoke until I recorded myself!

Presentation Skills Wrap-Up

Use Presentation Skills

Use the picture prompt to answer the questions.

1. You will tell a story about something that is happening in the picture.

   a. Identify the audience for your story. (Be imaginative! Feel free to pretend you're speaking to the Queen of England or to a room of preschoolers.)

   _____

   b. Identify the purpose of your story. Is it to entertain? To inform?

   _____

c. Given your audience and purpose, will you use formal or informal language? Explain.

_____

_____

_____

_____

2. Write notes that you can use as you tell the story. You may include details that are not shown in the picture. Have fun with it!

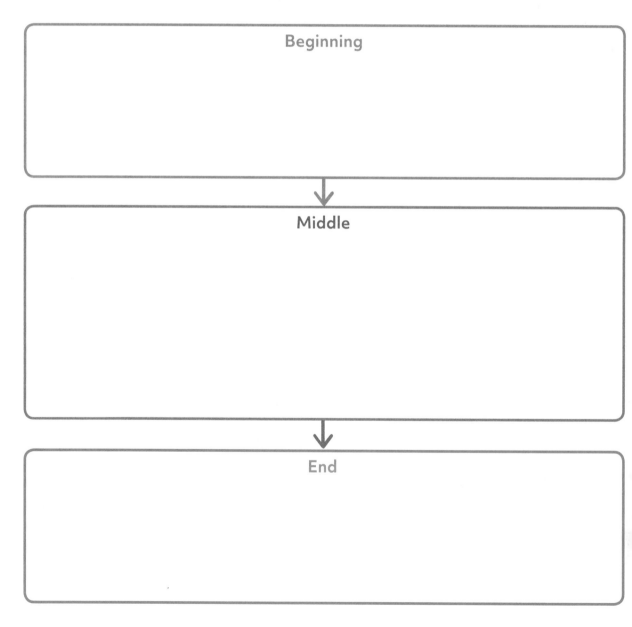

Beginning

Middle

End

3. Record your speech.

   • Use formal or informal language depending on your audience and purpose.

   • Refer to your graphic organizer from Question 2 as you speak.

   • Speak clearly and at an understandable pace.

4. Listen to your speech.

   a. Describe two strengths of your speech.

   _____

   _____

   _____

   b. Describe two ways you could improve your speech.

   _____

   _____

   _____

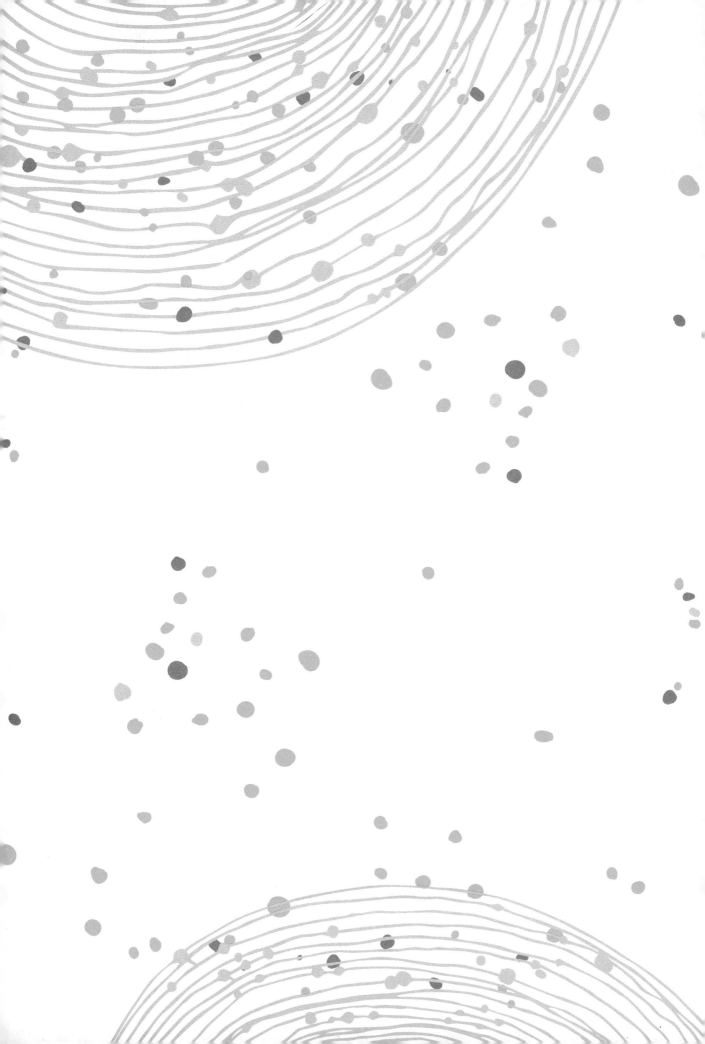

"Why Kids Should Eat Healthy and Exercise"

Spelling List 22 Pretest

1. **Open the Spelling Pretest activity online. Listen to the first spelling word. Type the word. Check your answer.**

2. **Write the correct spelling of the word in the Word column of the Spelling Pretest table on the next page.**

	Word	✓	✗
1	blindfold		

3. **Put a check mark in the ✓ column if you spelled the word correctly online.**

	Word	✓	✗
1	blindfold	✓	

   Put an X in the ✗ column if you spelled the word incorrectly online.

	Word	✓	✗
1	blindfold		X

4. **Repeat Steps 1–3 for the remaining words in the Spelling Pretest.**

"WHY KIDS SHOULD EAT HEALTHY AND EXERCISE" **375**

"Why Kids Should Eat Healthy and Exercise"

Spelling List 22 Pretest

Write each spelling word in the Word column, making sure to spell it correctly.

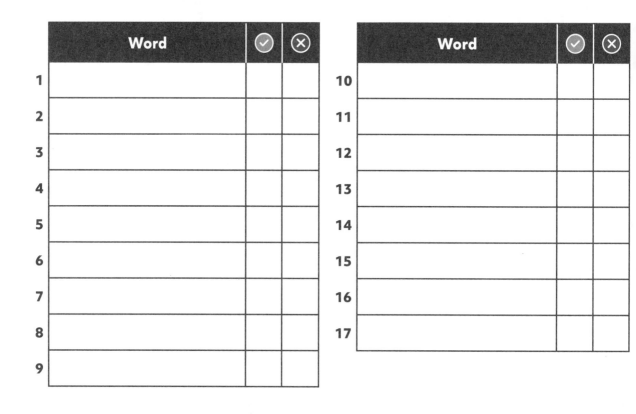

	Word	✓	✗
1			
2			
3			
4			
5			
6			
7			
8			
9			

	Word	✓	✗
10			
11			
12			
13			
14			
15			
16			
17			

"Why Kids Should Eat Healthy and Exercise"

Plan a Media Message

Use the prompt to answer the questions.

Prompt: **Create a media message on a topic of your choice.**
This video should share an important message for kids.
Note: You will not actually create this video.

1. Choose a topic for your media message. Choose from the following topics or come up with a topic of your own.

   - The best sport to play is [name of sport].

   - Why [name of food] is healthy food choice

   - Why a [name of animal] is a good pet

The topic of my media message will be

_____

_____

2. What is the main point, or the main idea, that you want to convey in your media message?

_____

_____

3. Complete the chart. List three details that support your media message. Describe video images that support each detail.

Supporting Details	Video Images for Supporting Detail
Supporting Detail 1	
Supporting Detail 2	
Supporting Detail 3	

"Why Kids Should Eat Healthy and Exercise" Wrap-Up

Spelling List 22 Activity Bank

Circle any words in the box that you did not spell correctly on the pretest. Using your circled words, complete one activity of your choice. Complete as much of the activity as you can in the time given.

If you spelled all words correctly on the pretest, complete your chosen activity with as many spelling words as you can.

annoy	employ	royal	form	formula
coil	exploit	voyage	formal	Maryland
coinage	ointment	conform	deform	Oregon
disappoint	poison			

Spelling Activity Choices

Hidden Words

1. Draw a picture and "hide" as many words from the Spelling Word List inside the picture as you can.

2. See if others can find the words within the picture.

Triangle Spelling

Write each word in a triangle.

d
do
dog

Ghost Words

1. Use a white crayon to write each spelling word.

2. Go over the white crayon writing with a colored marker.

Complete the activity that you chose.

My chosen activity: _____

"Why Kids Should Eat Healthy and Exercise" Wrap-Up

Write a Script for a Media Message

Use the prompt to answer the questions.

Prompt: **Create a media message on a topic of your choice.
This video should share an important message for kids.**
Note: You will not actually create this video.

1. What will be the title of your media message?

2. Plan the introduction to your media message. Be sure to have the narrator state the main point you wish to convey in the video. If you wish, write the script with yourself as the narrator.

What will the introduction title card say?

What will the narrator say?

What images will be in this section of the video?

3. Plan the supporting details of your media message. Again, you may imagine yourself as the narrator.

What will the title card for Detail 1 say?

_____

What will the narrator say?   What images will appear?

_____   _____

_____   _____

_____   _____

_____   _____

_____   _____

What will the title card for Detail 2 say?

_____

What will the narrator say?   What images will appear?

_____   _____

_____   _____

_____   _____

_____   _____

_____   _____

What will the title card for Detail 3 say?

_____

What will the narrator say?

_____

_____

_____

_____

_____

What images will appear?

_____

_____

_____

_____

_____

Personally, I think more people should adopt cats.

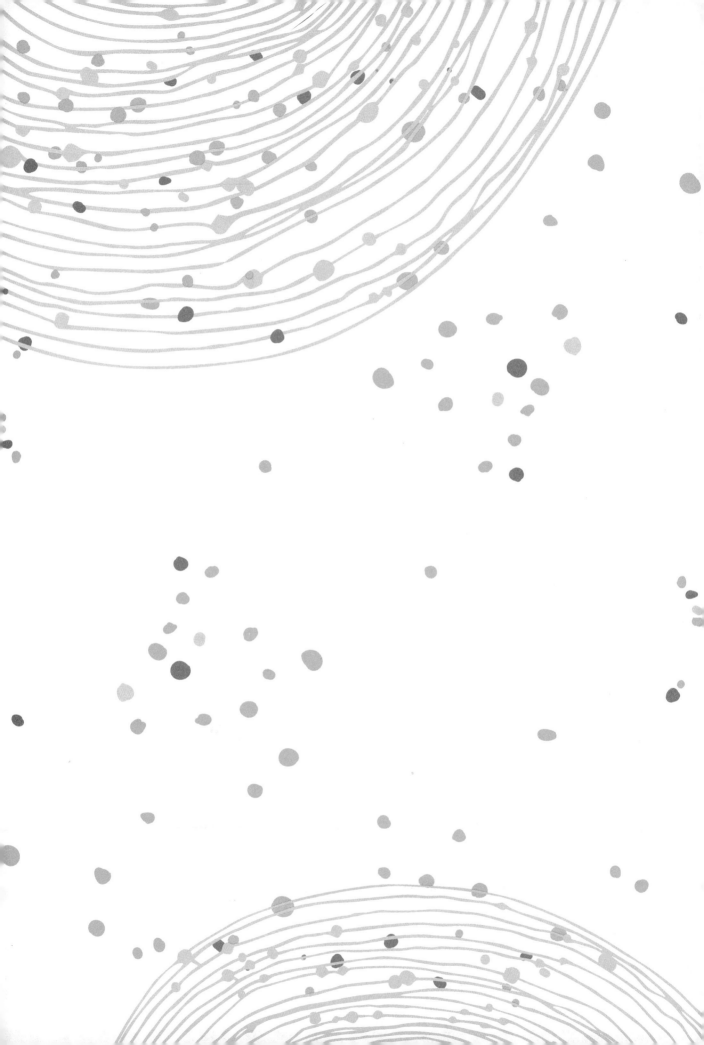

Staying Safe While Being Active

Write About Safety Equipment

Refer to the Safety Equipment web page for information. Then answer the questions, using complete sentences in your responses.

1. What is the best way to get to the information about each piece of safety equipment described on the web page? Explain why that is the best way.

2. Think about making your own safety web page. Name a sport or activity that you participate in or that you would like to participate in. Write a paragraph that explains which items of safety equipment you should wear for that sport or activity and how each piece of equipment would protect you.

Staying Safe While Being Active Wrap-Up

Design a Web Page

Answer the questions. Then use your answers to plan a web page that explains how to stay safe when participating in your favorite sport or activity.

1. What is your favorite sport or physical activity to participate in?

_____

2. List the types of safety equipment you need for this sport or activity.

_____

_____

3. Is anything else necessary to be safe for this sport or activity?

_____

_____

4. Use the box provided to plan a web page that tells about your favorite sport or activity and how you stay safe while participating in it. Be sure to include a visual element, such as a diagram, that would include links. Identify items that would be links with a capital letter L. Note that a website title and navigation bar have been provided for you. Write the title of your web page below the navigation bar, and add the name of your activity to the navigation bar.

myfavoriteactivities.com

Soccer   Basketball   Swimming   My activity: _____

Web page title: _____

Keeping Safe From Rabies

Spelling List 23 Pretest

1. Open the Spelling Pretest activity online. Listen to the first spelling word. Type the word. Check your answer.

2. Write the correct spelling of the word in the Word column of the Spelling Pretest table on the next page.

Word	✓	✗
1 blindfold		

3. Put a check mark in the ✓ column if you spelled the word correctly online.

Put an X in the ✗ column if you spelled the word incorrectly online.

Word	✓	✗
1 blindfold	✓	

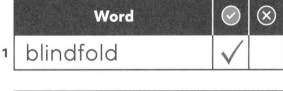

Word	✓	✗
1 blindfold		X

4. Repeat Steps 1–3 for the remaining words in the Spelling Pretest.

Keeping Safe From Rabies

Spelling List 23 Pretest

Write each spelling word in the Word column, making sure to spell it correctly.

	Word	✓	✕
1			
2			
3			
4			
5			
6			
7			
8			
9			
10			
11			
12			
13			

	Word	✓	✕
14			
15			
16			
17			
18			
19			
20			
21			
22			
23			
24			
25			

Keeping Safe from Rabies

Write About the Main Idea and Supporting Details

On the home page of the Rabies website, select the link for the web page "How do you know if an animal has rabies?" Read the information on the web page, and use it to write a response in complete sentences.

Write a paragraph that states the main idea and supporting details of the text on the web page that answers the question "How do you know if an animal has rabies?"

_____

_____

_____

_____

_____

_____

_____

_____

_____

_____

_____

_____

_____

I learned a lot about rabies from this website.

Keeping Safe from Rabies Wrap-Up

Spelling List 23 Activity Bank

Circle any words in the box that you did not spell correctly on the pretest. Using your circled words, complete one activity of your choice. Complete as much of the activity as you can in the time given.

If you spelled all words correctly on the pretest, complete your chosen activity with as many spelling words as you can.

allow	drowsy	howling	various	awareness
blouse	bounced	vowels	victorious	closeness
bound	rowdy	cloudy	harmonious	forgiveness
clownish	scoundrel	furious	Florida	goodness
drown	surround	glorious	Nebraska	illness

Spelling Activity Choices

Create a Crossword

1. Write a word from your spelling word list in the center of the grid paper.

2. Write another spelling word going across and sharing a letter with the first word. See how many words you can connect.

Example:

			p			
	k	i	s	s	e	s
d		n				
r	o	c	k	s		
g						
s						

Word Search Puzzle

1. Draw a box on the grid paper. The box should be large enough to hold your words from the spelling word list.

2. Fill in the grid paper with words from your spelling list, writing them horizontally, vertically, and diagonally (forward and backward if you choose).

3. Fill in the rest of the box with random letters.

4. Ask someone to find and circle your spelling words in the puzzle you made.

Complete the activity that you chose.

My chosen activity: _____

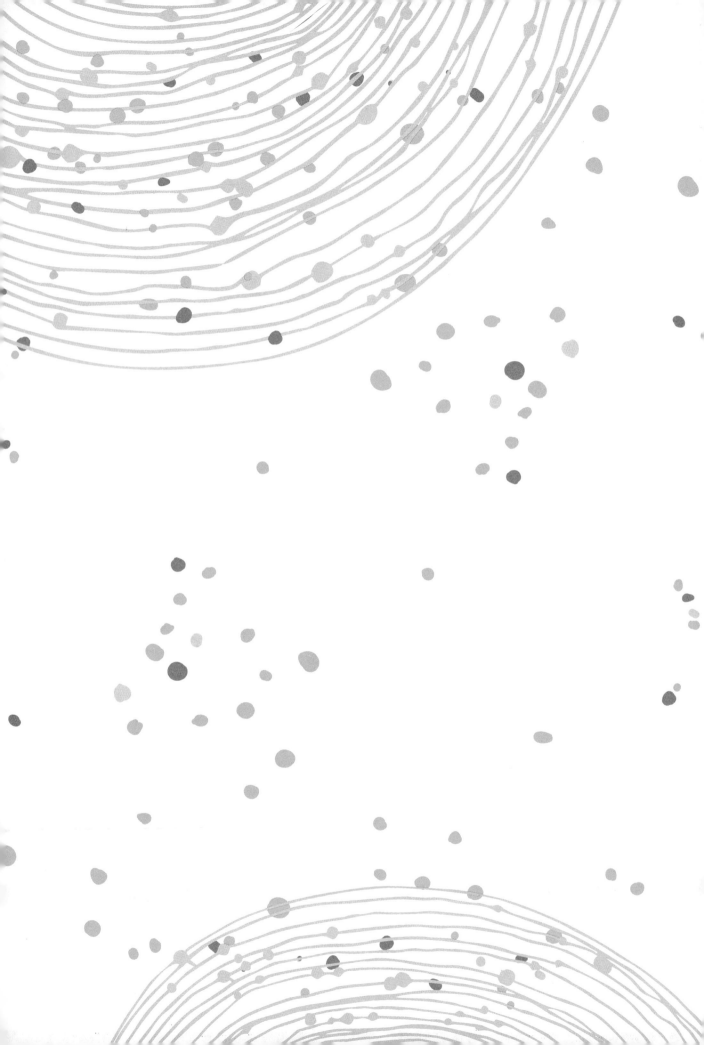

Keeping Safe from Rabies Wrap-Up

Make a Flyer About the Rabies Virus

On the home page of the Rabies website, select the Rabies Virus link. Read the information on the web page, and use it to create a flyer.

Plan out a flyer that informs people about rabies — what causes it and how it spreads. Your flyer can be as creative as you like, but it must include the main idea and supporting details of the text on the Rabies Virus web page. Use the space to take notes from the website for your flyer.

Prepare to Write a Primary Source of Information

An autobiography is a primary source of information. Prepare to write a brief autobiography about yourself by completing the graphic organizer.

Facts About Me

I am _____ years old.

My birthday is

_____ .

Where I was born:

_____

Family members:

_____

_____

_____

Friends:

_____

_____

_____

My Favorite Activity

Something I love to do is

_____

_____

My Favorite Things

Food:

_____

Movie:

_____

Book:

_____

Sport:

_____

Singer or Song:

_____

Interesting Facts

Two things I'd like you to know about me:

_____

_____

_____

_____

The Best Thing

The best thing that ever happened to me:

_____

_____

_____

_____

_____

Elizabeth Blackwell Wrap-Up

Write Your Autobiography

Gather the activity book page Prepare to Write a Primary Source of Information from Elizabeth Blackwell. Use the information recorded on the activity book page to complete the following tasks. Use complete sentences in your response.

1. Use the information in the Facts About Me box to write 3–4 sentences that introduce your autobiography.

2. Use the information in the Favorite Things and My Favorite Activity boxes to write 3–4 sentences.

_____

_____

_____

_____

_____

_____

_____

_____

_____

_____

_____

3. Use the information in the Interesting Facts box to write 3–4 sentences.

_____

_____

_____

_____

_____

_____

_____

_____

4. Use the information in The Best Thing box to write 3–4 sentences.

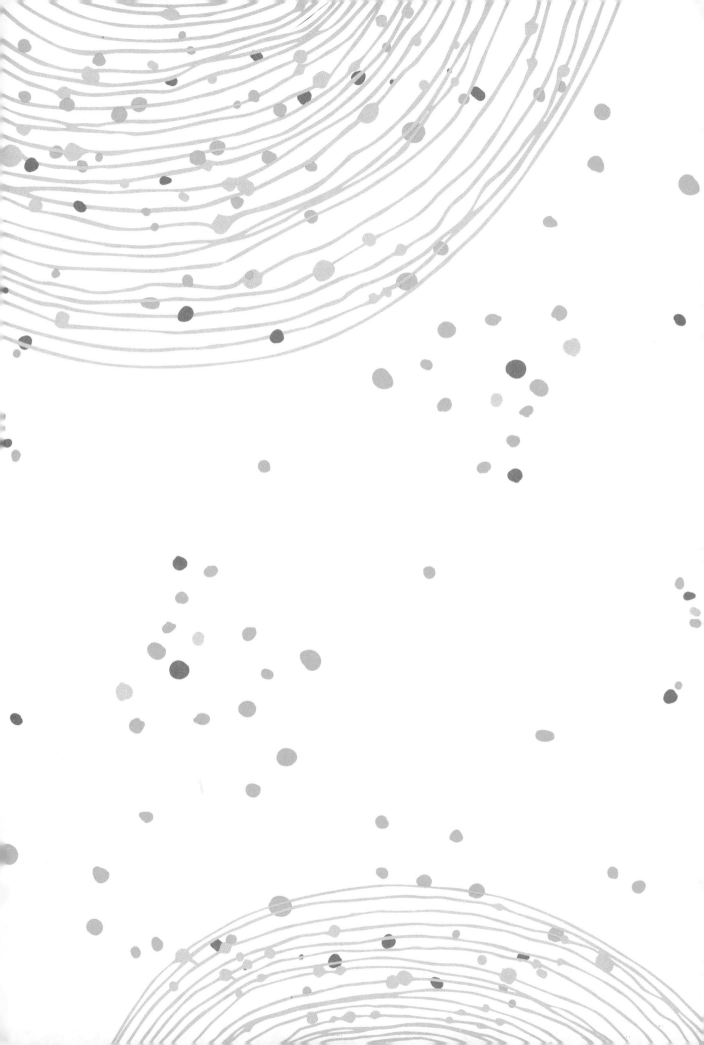

Write to Clarify the Meaning

Rewrite the following sentences from the story or add a second
sentence to clarify the meaning of the word or phrase in bold type.
The first one has been done for you.

1. Some found **shelter**.

    New sentence: Some found **shelter**, running into any house
    to hide behind the protection of a door.

2. **Panic-stricken** people scattered before it.

    _____

    _____

    _____

3. One day he was in his **laboratory** with his assistant.

    _____

    _____

    _____

4. Once more, the laboratory door **burst open** and Madame Meister
    stood there.

    _____

    _____

    _____

5. During this time, the person's body would be building up **resistance**.

_____

_____

_____

"Louis Pasteur: Battle with Death" Wrap-Up

Write a Summary of "Louis Pasteur: Battle with Death"

Answer the question, then write a summary of "Louis Pasteur: Battle with Death." Use complete sentences in your summary.

1. Which statement is the main idea of "Louis Pasteur: Battle with Death"?

   a. Louis Pasteur was haunted his whole life by the memory of a rabid wolf attacking people in his village.

   b. Louis Pasteur grew up to be a scientist whose work led to the prevention of many diseases, including rabies.

   c. Louis Pasteur spent many long hours developing a 14-day treatment that cured rabies.

2. Write a summary of "Louis Pasteur: Battle with Death." Be sure to include the main idea of the story and details that support the main idea.

_____

_____

_____

_____

_____

_____

_____

_____

_____

_____

_____

Greek Affixes

Apply: Greek Affixes

Rewrite the following sentences or add additional sentences to give a context clue for each vocabulary word's meaning. The first one has been done for you.

1. The room is **monochrome**.

   New sentence: The room is **monochrome**. All the walls and furniture are yellow.

2. My dad just bought an electric **automobile**.

   _____

   _____

   _____

   _____

   _____

3. I read the **autobiography** of the man who invented the stoplight.

   _____

   _____

   _____

   _____

   _____

4. Jacob asked his favorite author for his **autograph**.

_____

_____

_____

_____

_____

Answer the question. Use a vocabulary word in your response, and be sure to include enough context so a reader could determine the meaning of the word. Use complete sentences in your response.

5. Which would you rather have, a famous movie star's **autograph** or **autobiography**?

_____

_____

_____

_____

_____

Marine Biology Words

Apply: Marine Biology Words

Create a definition of each word or phrase. Use your knowledge of its root, any prefixes or suffixes it contains, and context clues to help you.

Focus Word: **marine** – (adj.) relating to the ocean or water

1. Word: **submarine**

   The large **submarine** went quickly through the dark waters. The people on board were eager to get back on land because they had been underwater for more than six months.

   I know that marine means "relating to the ocean or water." So, a submarine is

2. Word: **aquamarine**

   That ring is beautiful! The **aquamarine** stone reminds me of the blue and green water in the Bahamas.

   I know that marine means "relating to the ocean or water." So, aquamarine is

3. Word: **marine life**

   I find animals that live in the ocean to be fascinating. **Marine life** has so many bright colors and such interesting patterns.

   I know that marine means "relating to the ocean or water." So, marine life is

Focus Phrase: **tide pool** – (n.) a pool of sea water left behind when the tide goes out

4. Phrase: **tide line**

   Every morning I walk on the beach at the **tide line**. It is interesting to see the highest point of the tide.

   I know that tide pool is a pool of sea water left behind when the tide goes out. So, a tide line is

5. Phrase: **tide gate**

   The **tide gate** helps keep the water from flooding our area when it is high tide.

   I know that a tide pool is a pool of sea water left behind when the tide goes out. So, a tide gate is

Presentation: Digital Tools

Spelling List 24 Pretest

1. Open the Spelling Pretest activity online. Listen to the first spelling word. Type the word. Check your answer.

2. Write the correct spelling of the word in the Word column of the Spelling Pretest table on the next page.

Word	✓	✗
1 blindfold		

3. Put a check mark in the ✓ column if you spelled the word correctly online.

Word	✓	✗
1 blindfold	✓	

   Put an X in the ✗ column if you spelled the word incorrectly online.

Word	✓	✗
1 blindfold		✗

4. Repeat Steps 1–3 for the remaining words in the Spelling Pretest.

Presentation: Digital Tools

Spelling List 24 Pretest

Write each spelling word in the Word column, making sure to spell it correctly.

	Word	✓	✗
1			
2			
3			
4			
5			
6			
7			
8			
9			
10			
11			

	Word	✓	✗
12			
13			
14			
15			
16			
17			
18			
19			
20			
21			

Presentation: Digital Tools

Use Presentation Software

Use presentation software to complete this activity.

1. Open the presentation software and select **Blank Presentation**.

2. Go to **File > Save As**, and select a location on your computer in which to save your presentation. Give your presentation a name. Do not delete the file extension (for example, ".pptx") from your name.

3. Create the slides of your presentation.

   a. **Slide 1:** Add a title to the first slide of your presentation. The title can be anything you like (for example, "Gymnastics"). If you wish, add a subtitle.

   b. **Slide 2:** Select **New Slide** from the Home tab to create a second slide. Add a title and at least two bullets with text next to them to your slide. Your bullets should relate to your title.

   c. **Slide 3:** Select **New Slide** to create a third slide. Add a title to your slide. Then add a picture by selecting the Pictures icon on the slide or by going to **Insert > Pictures**. Select a picture that is on your computer (for example, a picture from the Sample Pictures folder). If you can't find a picture that relates to your title, that's okay.

   d. **Slide 4:** Select **New Slide** to create a fourth slide. Add a title to your slide. Then go to **Insert > Audio > Record Audio**. Press the record button (a red circle), and talk for about twenty seconds. When you're finished recording, press the stop button (a blue square). Then press OK. Move the speaker icon next to the title. If you wish, add bullets and text to the slide.

4. Select **Slide Show > From Beginning**. Review your presentation!

5. Save your presentation to your computer using **File > Save** or the Save icon.

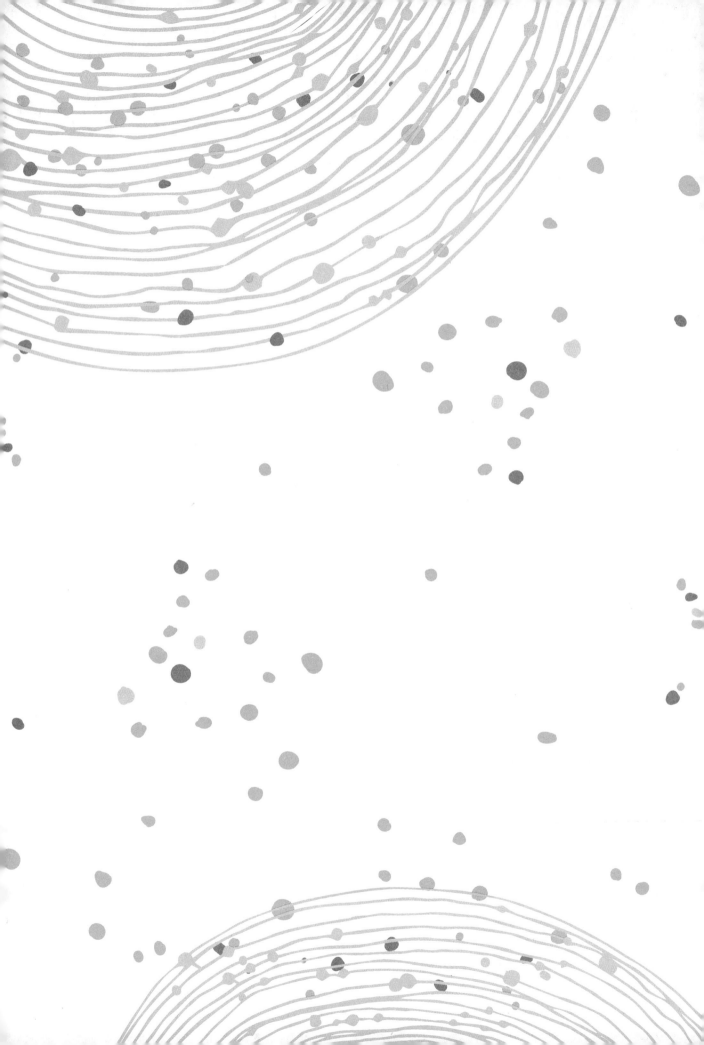

Presentation: Planning

Spelling List 24 Activity Bank

Circle any words in the box that you did not spell correctly on the pretest. Using your circled words, complete one activity of your choice. Complete as much of the activity as you can in the time given.

If you spelled all words correctly on the pretest, complete your chosen activity with as many spelling words as you can.

apprentice	novice	lattice	tension	desirous
furnace	palace	terrace	tent	famous
justice	surface	antenna	North Dakota	nervous
menace	service	extend	Utah	ridiculous
notice				

Spelling Activity Choices

Vowel-Free Words

1. In the left column, write only the consonants in each word and put a dot where each vowel should be.

2. Spell each word out loud, stating which vowels should be in the places you wrote dots.

3. In the right column, rewrite the entire spelling word.

4. Correct any spelling errors.

Alphabetizing

1. In the left column, write your words from the spelling word list in alphabetical order.

2. Correct any spelling errors.

Parts of Speech

1. In the left column, write the words from your spelling list that are nouns.

2. In the right column, write all the other words from your spelling list and label each word's part of speech.

3. Correct any spelling errors.

Uppercase and Lowercase

1. In the left column, write each of your words in all capital (uppercase) letters.

2. In the right column, write each of your words in all lowercase letters.

3. Correct any spelling errors.

Complete the activity that you chose.

My chosen activity: _____

1. _____   _____

2. _____   _____

3. _____   _____

4. _____   _____

5. _____   _____

6. _____   _____

7. _____   _____

8. _____   _____

9. _____   _____

10. _____   _____

11. _____   _____

12. _____   _____

13. _____   _____

14. _____   _____

15. _____   _____

16. _____   _____

17. _____   _____

18. _____   _____

19. _____   _____

20. _____   _____

21. _____   _____

22. _____   _____

23. _____   _____

24. _____   _____

25. _____   _____

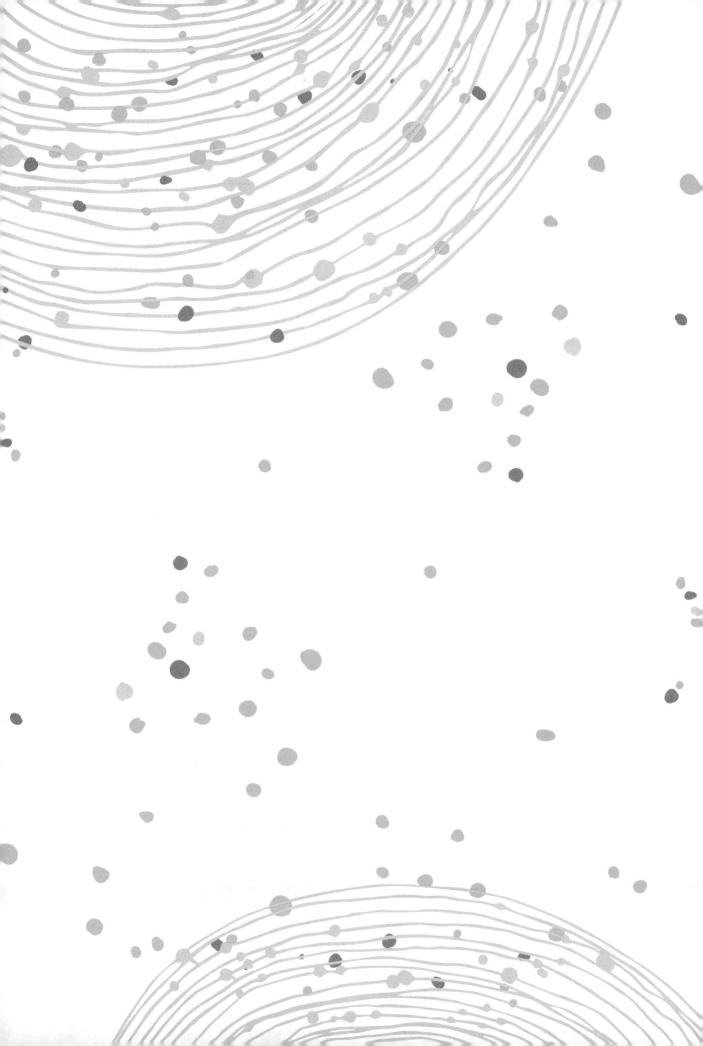

Presentation: Planning

Plan Your Presentation

Read the assignment. You will complete the assignment in steps over multiple lessons.

Prompt: **Use presentation software to create a public service announcement about a topic of your choice.**

Requirements:

Use the template provided to create the following slides:

- A **title** slide
- A **hook** slide that catches the audience's attention about your topic; includes a heading, picture, and audio
- An **introduction** slide that states your message and shows its importance; includes a heading, picture, and audio
- Three **body** slides each organized on a subtopic that provide facts and details that support your message; each slide includes a heading, bulleted talking points, a picture, and audio
- A **conclusion** slide that restates and emphasizes your message; includes a heading, picture, and audio
- A **sources** slide that lists at least two trustworthy research sources

Be sure to do the following:

- Speak clearly and at an appropriate pace.
- Include relevant information from your research and your personal experience.
- Include the **URLs** of any pictures used in the presentation that you found online.
- Use correct **grammar**, **usage**, and **mechanics**.

Audience: You will identify an appropriate audience for your presentation based on your message.

Purpose: Persuade your audience to listen to your message.

Brainstorm and choose a topic for your presentation.

1. Think about issues that are important to you. List as many topics as you can think of.

2. Read your answers to Question 1.

   a. Circle two topics that interest you the most.

   b. For each topic you chose, try stating a message related to the topic. Two sample topics and messages are shown.

Topic 1: litter from plastic water bottles

Message: Use a reusable water bottle instead of plastic water bottles.

Topic 2: animals in shelters

Message: Adopt a dog from a shelter instead of getting a dog from a breeder.

Topic 1:

_____

Message:

_____

_____

Topic 2:

_____

Message:

_____

_____

3. Decide which message you wrote in Question 2 interests you more. Then answer Yes or No to each question.

   a. Is your message something that can be covered well in a six-slide presentation? _____

   b. Is your message something you can expand upon with at least three supporting subtopics? _____

   c. Is your message something that you can support with research?

   _____

4. Did you answer Yes to Parts A–C of Question 3? You have found your presentation topic! If not, go back to the topics you listed in Question 1, choose a different topic, and follow the process described in Questions 2 and 3.

5. Think about your message. Who is the audience for your message? Explain. (The *actual* audience will be your teacher, but you should target an audience that you feel is appropriate for your message.)

   _____

   _____

   _____

6. The purpose of a public service announcement is to persuade your audience to listen to your message. Based on your audience and purpose, list three subtopics that best support your message. Your subtopics should help your audience understand and then agree with your message.

   _____

   _____

   _____

Presentation: Research

Research Your Presentation

Follow these steps to write research questions.

1. Write the message of your public service announcement.

   Sample message: Use a reusable water bottle instead of plastic water bottles.

   My message:

   _____

   _____

2. List at least three subtopics that will help your audience understand— and then agree with—your message. Write questions that you can research to find facts and details that support each subtopic.

Subtopic	Research Questions
Sample: Using plastic water bottles is more expensive than using a reusable water bottle.	Sample: How much does a plastic water bottle cost? How much money does a reusable water bottle cost? How long does a reusable water bottle last?

Subtopic	Research Questions

Follow these steps to conduct research. Record information on the Research Notes pages that follow. Use one page per source.

3. Identify at least two sources (digital, print, or both) that you can use to answer your research questions. Record the title, author, publisher, and URL of each source.

4. As you read each source, take notes related to your research questions.

    - Write your notes in your own words.

    - If you find a direct quotation that you think you might use in your report, record the quotation, word for word, in quotation marks. Also record the name of the person you are quoting.

It takes over 400 years for a plastic water bottle to decompose.

Research Notes

Source

Title: _____

Author: _____

Published by: _____

URL (if necessary): _____

Notes

Key Information Written in Your Own Words:

_____

_____

_____

_____

_____

_____

_____

Direct Quotation:

_____

_____

_____

Person Quoted: _____

Research Notes

Source

Title: _____

Author: _____

Published by: _____

URL (if necessary): _____

Notes

Key Information Written in Your Own Words:

_____

_____

_____

_____

_____

_____

_____

_____

Direct Quotation:

_____

_____

_____

Person Quoted: _____

Reflect on your research.

5. What general conclusions can you draw from your research? Summarize your research in 1 or 2 sentences.

_____

_____

_____

_____

6. Look back at your research questions.

   a. How well does your research answer each of your questions?

   _____

   _____

   _____

   _____

   b. Did you answer any questions that you didn't originally ask? If so, what?

   _____

   _____

   _____

   _____

   c. Based on your research, revise your subtopics, or even your message. If you don't have any revisions to make, explain why.

   _____

   _____

   _____

Coral Reefs (A)

Spelling List 25 Pretest

1. Open the Spelling Pretest activity online. Listen to the first spelling word. Type the word. Check your answer.

2. Write the correct spelling of the word in the Word column of the Spelling Pretest table on the next page.

3. Put a check mark in the ✓ column if you spelled the word correctly online.

   Put an X in the ✗ column if you spelled the word incorrectly online.

4. Repeat Steps 1–3 for the remaining words in the Spelling Pretest.

Coral Reefs (A)

Spelling List 25 Pretest

Write each spelling word in the Word column, making sure to spell it correctly.

	Word	✓	✕
1			
2			
3			
4			
5			
6			
7			
8			
9			
10			
11			

	Word	✓	✕
12			
13			
14			
15			
16			
17			
18			
19			
20			
21			

Write About Coral Reefs and Camouflage

Read the passage from *National Geographic: Coral Reefs* by Kristin Baird Rattini. Then answer the questions in complete sentences.

Many animals use camouflage (KAM-uh-flazh) to hide along the reef. Some use it to stay safe from other animals that could eat them. Others use it to hide while they hunt.

A stonefish's bumpy body blends in with the coral. A trumpetfish dives down and holds still. Its long, thin body stretches up like a tall sponge. A cuttlefish can change its shape and skin color to match the coral reef.

1. How does the coral reef benefit the sea animals in this ecosystem?

2. Write two details from the text that support your answer.

_____

_____

3. Make an inference: What would happen to the sea life if the coral reef did not exist? Be sure to include details that support your inference.

_____

_____

_____

_____

_____

_____

_____

Coral Reefs (B)

Spelling List 25 Activity Bank

Circle any words in the box that you did not spell correctly on the pretest. Using your circled words, complete one activity of your choice. Complete as much of the activity as you can in the time given.

If you spelled all words correctly on the pretest, complete your chosen activity with as many spelling words as you can.

couldn't	they're	you're	prefer	friendship
doesn't	who's	aren't	transfer	horsemanship
let's	won't	conference	Iowa	leadership
shouldn't	wouldn't	ferry	Michigan	relationship
there's				

Spelling Activity Choices

Silly Sentences

1. Write a silly sentence using your words from the spelling word list.

2. Underline the spelling word in each sentence.

   Example: The dog was <u>driving</u> a car.

3. Correct any spelling errors.

Spelling Story

1. Write a very short story using your words from the spelling word list.

2. Underline the spelling words in the story.

3. Correct any spelling errors.

Riddle Me This

1. Write a riddle for your words from the spelling word list.
   Example: "I have a trunk, but it's not on my car."

2. Write the answer, which is your word, for each riddle.
   Example: Answer: elephant

3. Correct any spelling errors.

RunOnWord

1. Gather some crayons, colored pencils, or markers. Write each of your words, using a different color for each word, end to end as one long word.
   Example: dogcatbirdfishturtle

2. Rewrite the words correctly and with proper spacing.

Complete the activity that you chose.

My chosen activity: _____

_____

_____

_____

_____

_____

_____

_____

_____

_____

_____

_____

_____

_____

_____

_____

_____

_____

_____

_____

_____

_____

_____

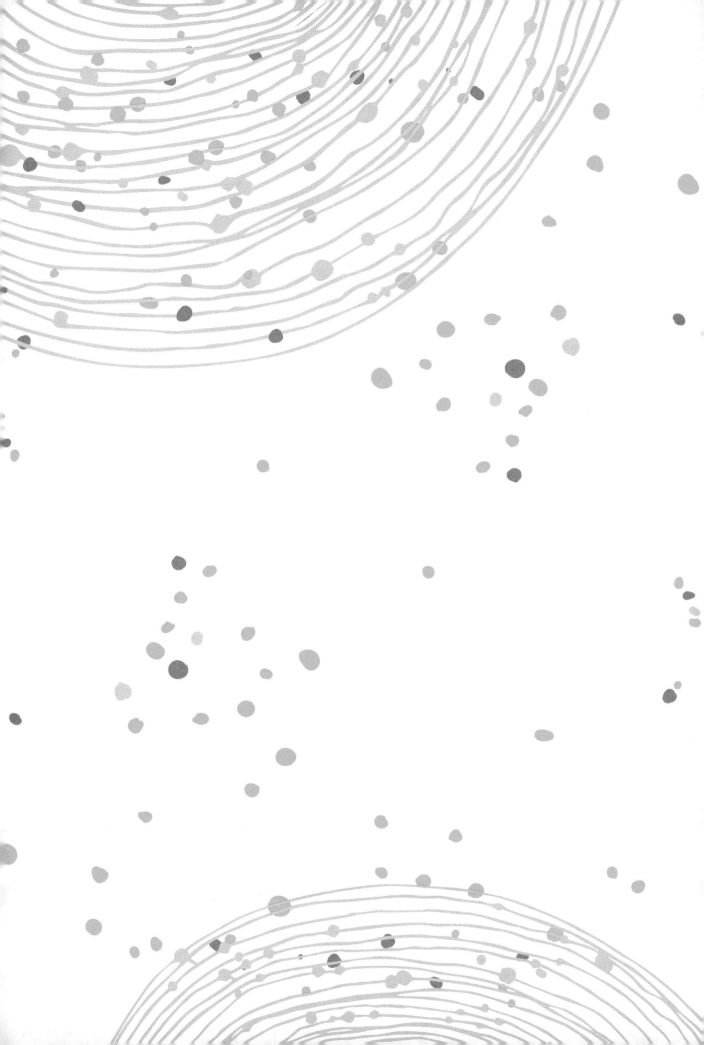

Coral Reefs (B)

Write About the Food Chain in Coral Reefs

Read the passage from *Who Eats What? Coral Reef Food Chains* by Rebecca Pettiford. Then answer the questions in complete sentences.

Plant plankton and sea grass are **producers**. They are the first link in the coral reef food chain. These plants use the sun's energy to make their own food.

Small fish and green sea turtles eat the plants. They are the next link in the chain. They are **consumers**.

Large fish, octopuses, and sharks eat consumers. They are **predators**, the next link in the chain.

Sharks are a top predator. They eat smaller predators.

When an animal dies, **decomposers** such as **bacteria** break down its body. They change the dead matter into **nutrients**. The nutrients return to the sea floor.

1. How do the parts of the coral reef food chain depend on each other? Include details from the text to support your answer.

Coral Reefs (C)

Write About Coral Reefs

Pretend you are being interviewed for a friend's project on marine life. Answer the questions about coral reefs using complete sentences. Be sure to use details from the different books you've read to support your answers.

1. Why are coral reefs so important?

_____

_____

_____

_____

_____

_____

_____

2. What are the top three facts you learned about coral reefs?

_____

_____

_____

_____

_____

_____

_____

3. How do coral reefs help animals and plants survive?

_____

_____

_____

_____

_____

_____

I would love to visit the Great Barrier Reef someday.

TRY IT

Coral Reefs (D)

Plan to Write a Persuasive Essay

Use the prompt to answer the questions.

Prompt: **Write a persuasive essay about an issue that's important to you.**

1. Brainstorm topics for your essay. List as many topics as you can in the box. Use these sentence starters to help you think of ideas:

   - I believe that . . .
   - It is important that . . .
   - Everyone should . . .
   - All children should be able to . . .

2. Read your list from Question 1 and choose a topic for your essay. Complete the sentence to clearly state the topic of your essay.

   I believe that _____ because

   _____

   _____ .

3. Who do you imagine as the audience of your persuasive essay? Why?

_____

_____

_____

4. List three reasons that support your opinion. For each reason, list supporting details. Choose reasons and details that will help you persuade your audience to agree with your opinion. You do not need to use complete sentences.

Reason 1:

_____

Supporting details:

_____

_____

_____

_____

Reason 2:

_____

Supporting details:

_____

_____

_____

_____

Reason 3:

_____

Supporting details:

_____

_____

_____

_____

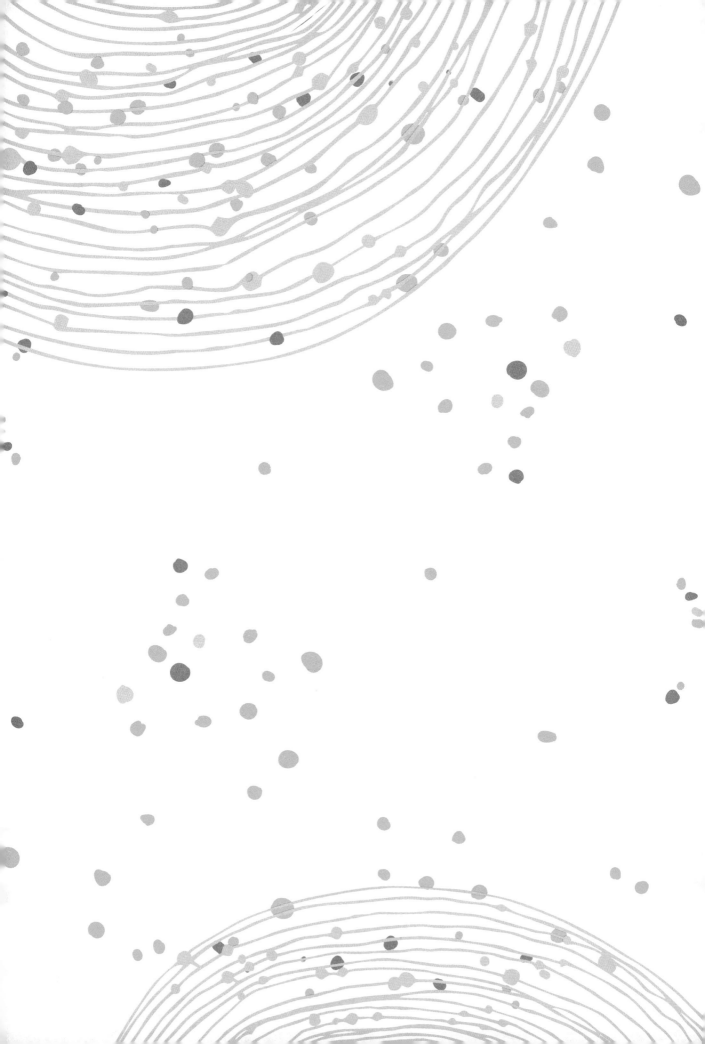

Coral Reefs Wrap-Up

Write a Persuasive Essay

Using your brainstorm as a guide, write a persuasive essay about an issue that's important to you.

Write your essay. Use the following structure:

- Paragraph 1: Hook your audience, clearly state your topic, and briefly state your supporting reasons.

- Paragraphs 2, 3, and 4: Write one paragraph about each supporting reason. Use details to support each reason.

- Paragraph 5: Briefly restate your topic and add any final thoughts.

Presentation: Revising

Revise Your Presentation

Use the checklist as you revise your public service announcement.

Content

☐ Hook: Will the hook capture the audience's attention?

☐ Introduction: Does the introduction state my message clearly?

☐ Body: Do the headings capture the main idea of each slide?

☐ Body: Is there information that I could add or delete to strengthen or clarify my message?

☐ Body: Do I include facts that I found during research? Do all of these facts support my message?

☐ Body: Did I use sensory details to paint a picture with words?

☐ Conclusion: Does the conclusion restate my message?

☐ Sources: Do I list two trustworthy research sources?

☐ Pictures: Do the pictures support the main idea of each slide?

☐ Pictures: Have I included the URL for any pictures that I found online?

Organization

☐ Does the order of the body slides make sense?

☐ Do the bullets support the main idea of each slide? Should any be moved to a different slide?

☐ Are the bullets in the same order in which I talk about them in the audio?

Presentation: Proofreading

Proofread Your Presentation

Use the checklist as you proofread the text and speech in your public service announcement. The items listed under Grammar and Usage apply to both text and speech.

Grammar and Usage

☐ Are all sentences complete and correct?

☐ Are there any missing or extra words?

☐ Are the words I use precise?

☐ Is the language appropriately formal or informal?

☐ Are there other grammatical or usage errors?

Mechanics

☐ Is every word spelled correctly, including frequently confused words?

☐ Does every sentence begin with a capital letter and end with the appropriate punctuation?

☐ Is punctuation used thoughtfully and effectively?

☐ Are the titles of works in the source list capitalized correctly?

☐ Are there other punctuation or capitalization errors?

Speech

- [ ] Do I speak at an appropriate pace? Are there any times I speak too quickly or too slowly?

- [ ] Do I speak clearly? Are there any words that I pronounce incorrectly?

- [ ] Do I speak at an appropriate volume?

Presentation: Publishing

Reflect on Your Presentation

Refer to your public service announcement as you answer the questions.

1. Who do you imagine as the audience for your public service announcement? Why?

   _____

   _____

   _____

   a. How did this audience influence the language you used in your public service announcement? Give at least one example.

   _____

   _____

   _____

   _____

   b. How did this audience influence what pictures or examples you used in your public service announcement? Give at least one example.

   _____

   _____

   _____

   _____

2. Suppose you wanted to share your public service announcement with the audience you named in Question 1. Where could you try to publish your public service announcement? Why?

Note: Because of potential image copyright issues, do not actually publish your public service announcement.

_____

_____

_____

_____

After answering these questions, I want to make a few tweaks to my PSA.

"Tayo's Wishes"

Spelling List 26 Pretest

1. Open the Spelling Pretest activity online. Listen to the first spelling word. Type the word. Check your answer.

2. Write the correct spelling of the word in the Word column of the Spelling Pretest table on the next page.

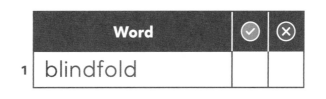

	Word	✓	✗
1	blindfold		

3. Put a check mark in the ✓ column if you spelled the word correctly online.

   Put an X in the ✗ column if you spelled the word incorrectly online.

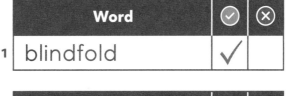

	Word	✓	✗
1	blindfold	✓	

	Word	✓	✗
1	blindfold		X

4. Repeat Steps 1–3 for the remaining words in the Spelling Pretest.

"Tayo's Wishes"

Spelling List 26 Pretest

Write each spelling word in the Word column, making sure to spell it correctly.

	Word	✓	✗
1			
2			
3			
4			
5			
6			
7			
8			
9			

	Word	✓	✗
10			
11			
12			
13			
14			
15			
16			
17			

Theme of a Legend

One theme of "Tayo's Wishes" is to be careful what you wish for because the results may not be what you expect. What is another possible theme of the text? Answer the questions using evidence from the text to guide you to another possible theme of "Tayo's Wishes."

1. How does Tayo feel when the people in the village call him "the hardest working man in all of Nigeria"?

2. Tayo makes a wish to have his work magically completed for him.

   a. At first, how does Tayo feel when he finds out his wish has come true?

   b. Then what happens?

3. Besides being careful about what you wish for, what else does Tayo learn?

_____

_____

_____

_____

_____

4. Based on what Tayo learns and your knowledge, what could be another theme of "Tayo's Wishes"?

_____

_____

_____

5. How does this theme apply to your life?

_____

_____

_____

"Tayo's Wishes" Wrap-Up

Spelling List 26 Activity Bank

Circle any words in the box that you did not spell correctly on the pretest. Using your circled words, complete one activity of your choice. Complete as much of the activity as you can in the time given.

If you spelled all words correctly on the pretest, complete your chosen activity with as many spelling words as you can.

anywhere	handshake	windshield	yardstick	Washington, D.C.
background	masterpiece	wristwatch	dishwasher	Puerto Rico
campground	overlook	toothpick	homesick	Guam
earthquake	supermarket			

Spelling Activity Choices

Hidden Words

1. Draw a picture and "hide" as many words from the Spelling Word List as they can inside the picture.

2. See if others can find the words within the picture.

Triangle Spelling

Write each word in a triangle.

d
do
dog

Ghost Words

1. Use a white crayon to write each spelling word.

2. Go over the white crayon writing with a colored marker.

Complete the activity that you chose.

My chosen activity: _____

"Tayo's Wishes" Wrap-Up

Analyze a Character

What kind of person is Tayo? Use the character traits from the word bank to describe Tayo throughout the story. Character traits may be used more than once.

Character Traits Word Bank

bossy	dependable	proud
brave	dishonest	responsible
clever	lazy	restless
kind	lonely	hardworking

Beginning	Middle	End

1. Describe Tayo using the words you selected and examples from the text to support your word selections.

_____

_____

_____

_____

_____

2. Does Tayo make you think of anyone you know? How is that person the same as Tayo? How is that person different from Tayo?

_____

_____

_____

_____

_____

"The Green Glass Ball"

Parts of a Drama

Read the excerpt of "The Green Ball."

"The Green Ball"

Cast of Characters

CASSIE, the talking dog

CONNOR, the boy

Present day, by the ocean

Scene 1

CONNOR: (*smiling*) Another beautiful day at the ocean, huh, Cassie?

CASSIE: (*jumping up and down*) Ruff, ruff! Yes, I love the beach so much! Can you throw the green ball please?

CONNOR: (*throws the ball*) Go, get it Cassie!

CASSIE: (*jumps into the water with a splash*) Oh, I love to swim! I love to swim! Hey, where did that ball go?

CONNOR: Cassie, where is that ball?

CASSIE: (*looking around the water*) I can't find it anywhere!

Answer the questions using complete sentences and the appropriate word from the word bank.

Parts of a Play Word Bank

cast of characters	description	stage directions
setting	dialogue	scenes

1. Who is in "The Green Ball"?

_____

2. Where does it take place?

_____

3. What is in parentheses ( )?

_____

   a. Why are stage directions needed in a play?

   _____

   _____

   _____

   b. What information do we learn about Cassie from the stage directions?

   _____

   _____

   _____

c. What information do we learn about Connor from the stage directions?

_____

_____

_____

What happens next? Continue the play in your own words. Write four lines that include stage directions for Cassie and Connor.

_____

_____

_____

_____

_____

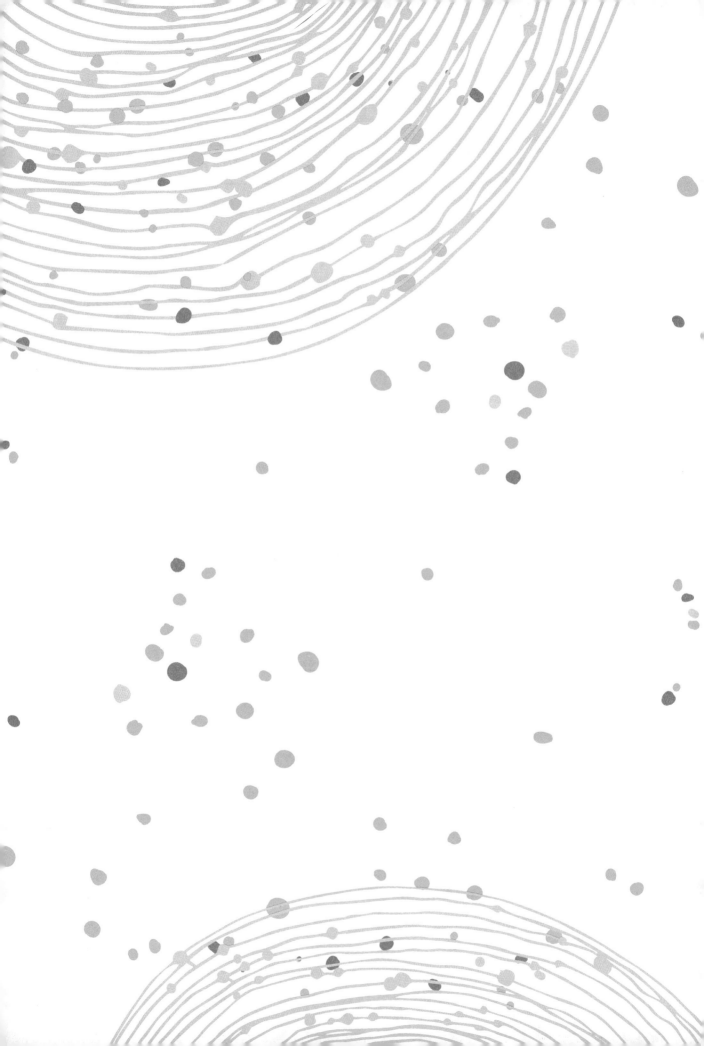

"The Green Glass Ball" Wrap-Up

Write About How Characters Change

In stories or plays, characters often change from beginning to end. How does Donkey in "The Green Glass Ball" change? Use the chart below to brainstorm about Donkey's changes and evidence from the text to support your ideas. The first one has been done for you.

Text Evidence	Notes About Donkey
Beginning "All you have to do is stroll around without a care in the world while I have to carry a heavy pack."	**Beginning** Is annoyed he does all the work
Beginning	**Beginning**
End	**End**
End	**End**

Explain how Donkey changes from beginning to end. Use evidence from the text to support your explanation.

_____

_____

_____

_____

_____

_____

_____

_____

_____

_____

_____

_____

_____

_____

_____

_____

_____

_____

_____

_____

Sometimes I think about how much I have changed over time.

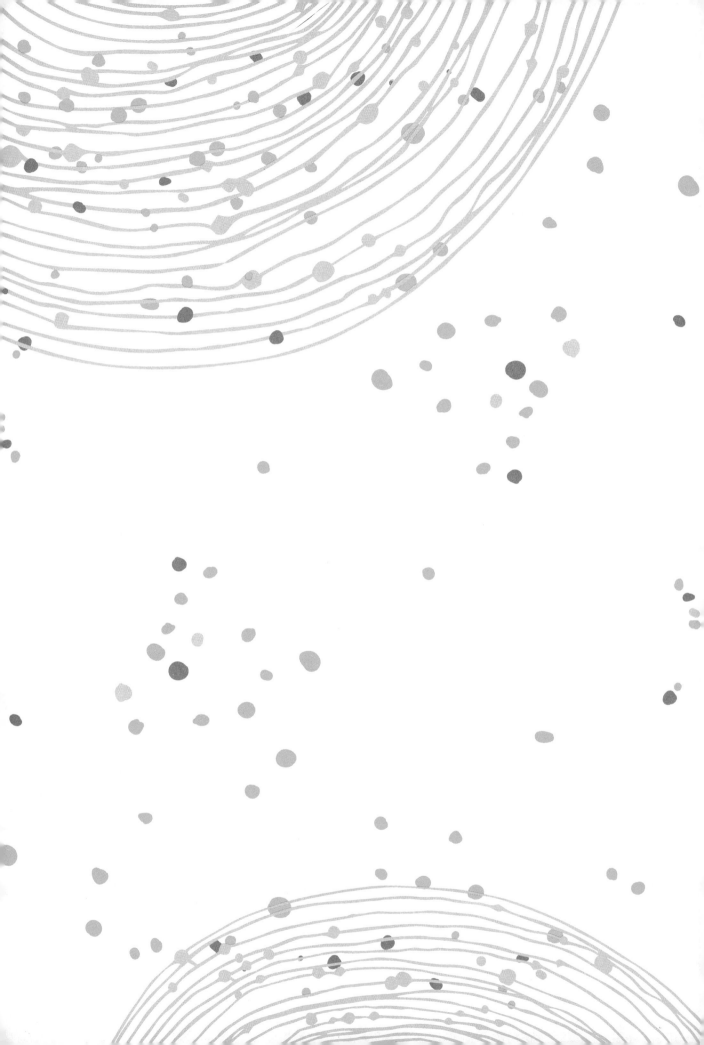

"The Gold Coin"

Spelling List 27 Pretest

1. Open the Spelling Pretest activity online. Listen to the first spelling word. Type the word. Check your answer.

2. Write the correct spelling of the word in the Word column of the Spelling Pretest table on the next page.

Word	✓	✗
1 blindfold		

3. Put a check mark in the ✓ column if you spelled the word correctly online.

Word	✓	✗
1 blindfold	✓	

Put an X in the ✗ column if you spelled the word incorrectly online.

Word	✓	✗
1 blindfold		✗

4. Repeat Steps 1–3 for the remaining words in the Spelling Pretest.

"The Gold Coin"

Spelling List 27 Pretest

Write each spelling word in the Word column, making sure to spell it correctly.

	Word	✓	✗
1			
2			
3			
4			
5			
6			
7			
8			
9			

	Word	✓	✗
10			
11			
12			
13			
14			
15			
16			
17			

TRY IT

"The Gold Coin"

Developing a Character

Read the passage. Then answer the questions to determine how the author of "The Gold Coin" develops the character of Doña Josefa. Use complete sentences in your responses.

> What was that shining in her hand? Juan wondered. He could not believe his eyes: It was a gold coin. Then he heard the woman say to herself, "I must be the richest person in the world."

1. Based on the passage, what does Juan believe about Doña Josefa?

2. Is Doña Josefa truly rich? How many gold coins does she have?

3. After the events of the passage above, Doña Josefa leaves with two men. When does she next appear in the story? How much time has passed between the events of the passage and when she next appears in the story?

Read the passage, and then answer the questions.

"…I went for her because my wife had been running a high fever. In no time at all, Doña Josefa had her on the road to recovery. And what's more, my friend, she brought her a gold coin!"

Juan groaned inwardly. To think that someone could hand out gold so freely! What a strange woman Doña Josefa is, Juan thought. Not only is she willing to help one person after another, but she doesn't mind traveling all over the countryside to do it!

4. What does this passage tell us about Doña Josefa?

5. Is Doña Josefa present when the man tells Juan how she helped his wife?

6. How do we learn what Doña Josefa is like when she isn't present for most of the story's events?

_____

_____

_____

_____

7. Write a paragraph that describes what Doña Josefa is like. Be sure to use examples of her actions in the story to support your description.

_____

_____

_____

_____

_____

_____

_____

_____

_____

_____

_____

_____

_____

_____

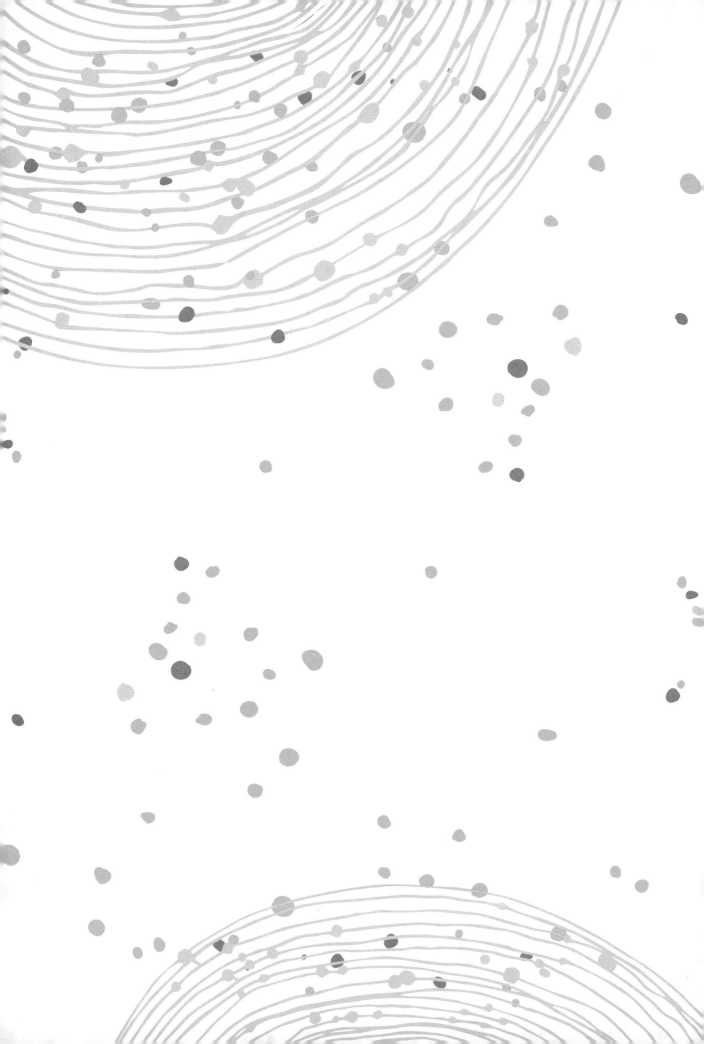

"The Gold Coin" Wrap-Up

Spelling List 27 Activity Bank

Circle any words in the box that you did not spell correctly on the pretest. Using your circled words, complete one activity of your choice. Complete as much of the activity as you can in the time given.

If you spelled all words correctly on the pretest, complete your chosen activity with as many spelling words as you can.

berry	mail	waist	lesson	rowed
bury	male	waste	road	close
groan	tail	lessen	rode	clothes
grown	tale			

Spelling Activity Choices

Create a Crossword

1. Write a word from your spelling word list in the center of the grid paper.

2. Write another spelling word going across and sharing a letter with the first word. See how many words you can connect.

Example:

			p			
		k	i	s	s	e	s
	d		n			
r	o	c	k	s		
	g					
	s					

Word Search Puzzle

1. Draw a box on the grid paper. The box should be large enough to hold your words from the spelling word list.

2. Fill in the grid paper with words from your spelling list, writing them horizontally, vertically, and diagonally (forward and backward if you choose).

3. Fill in the rest of the box with random letters.

4. Ask someone to find and circle your spelling words in the puzzle you made.

Complete the activity that you chose.

My chosen activity: _____

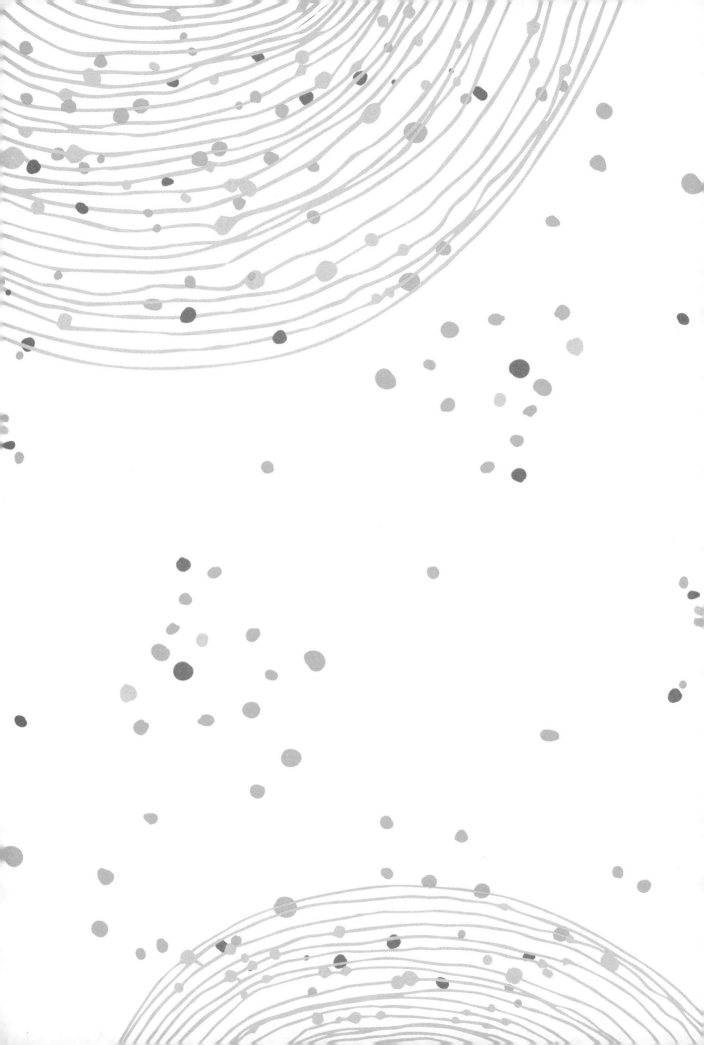

"The Gold Coin" Wrap-Up

Compare and Contrast Events

Summarize the main events of "The Gold Coin." Use the table to help you.

"The Gold Coin"	
Introduction	
Event 1	
Event 2	
Event 3	
Conclusion	

Read the summary of "The Green Glass Ball."

Tinker and Donkey go into town searching for work. In town, Tinker meets different people and helps them by fixing all sorts of objects. Instead of getting money for his work, he receives food. The last person he helps is an old woman. He fixes her kettle, and she pays him with a green glass ball. With the magical green glass ball, he can make a wish. Tinker and Donkey brainstorm different ideas and accidentally, in a moment of anger, Tinker wishes that Donkey would disappear, and he does. Tinker's nephew, Tim, uses the ball to make a wish to bring Donkey back. Tinker and Donkey forgive each other, and the old woman returns to take the ball. She reminds them to always make wishes that are kind and generous and to never make a mean wish.

Compare and contrast the events of "The Green Glass Ball" and "The Gold Coin."

1. What is the same about the events of "The Green Glass Ball" and "The Gold Coin"?

2. What is different about the events of "The Green Glass Ball" and "The Gold Coin"?

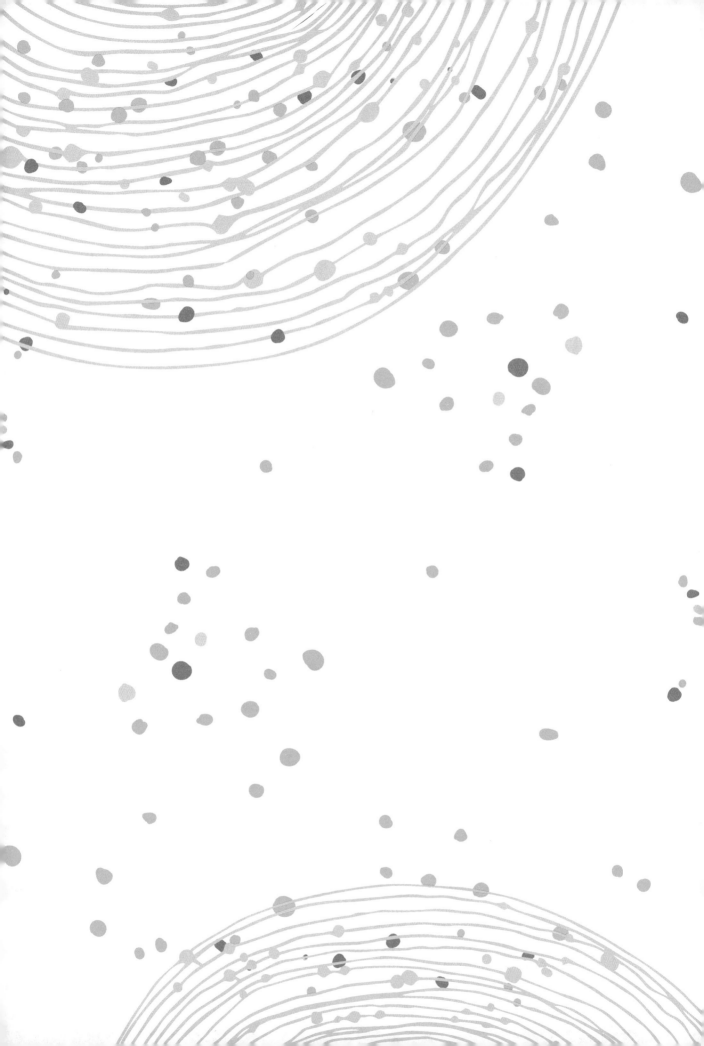

TRY IT

"The Grateful Stork"

Compare and Contrast Themes

Read possible themes from other texts in this unit. Then add a possible theme for "The Grateful Stork" to the last line of the chart.

Text	Possible Themes
"Tayo's Wishes"	Wishes can have unexpected results.
"The Green Glass Ball"	Happiness doesn't come from having wishes granted.
"The Gold Coin"	Happiness comes from acts of kindness and generosity.
"The Grateful Stork"	

1. Describe the similarities of the themes from "The Grateful Stork" and "The Gold Coin."

_____

_____

_____

_____

_____

2. Describe the differences between the themes of "The Grateful Stork" and "The Gold Coin."

"The Grateful Stork" Wrap-Up

Characters' Relationships Change

Cite evidence from the text and take notes about how the relationship between the old woman and the young girl changes in the "The Grateful Stork." The first note has been done for you. When you have completed the notes, write one page that describes the changes in their relationship.

Evidence	Notes
"Come in, come in," the old woman urged. "You must be terribly cold."	Shows how thoughtful and concerned the old woman is for the stranger (a young girl) that shows up at their door
"My, you are such a help to me!" she [the old woman] said over and over again.	
"You have made us happier than we can say," they answered to the young girl. "From this day on, we will love you and care for your as if you were our very own."	

Evidence	Notes
"No matter what happens, we will not look behind the screen while you are weaving."	
"I wanted to repay you for saving my life, so I decided to become a young girl and bring good fortune to your lives. But now I can no longer stay, for this morning Obaa-san saw me in my true form, and now you know my disguise."	
"Please forgive me," she murmured. "I was so anxious to see how you wove your cloth, I broke my promise to you and am very much ashamed."	

How does the relationship between the old woman and the young girl change? Write one page that includes examples from the story.

_____

_____

_____

_____

_____

_____

_____

_____

_____

_____

_____

_____

_____

_____

_____

_____

_____

_____

_____

_____

_____

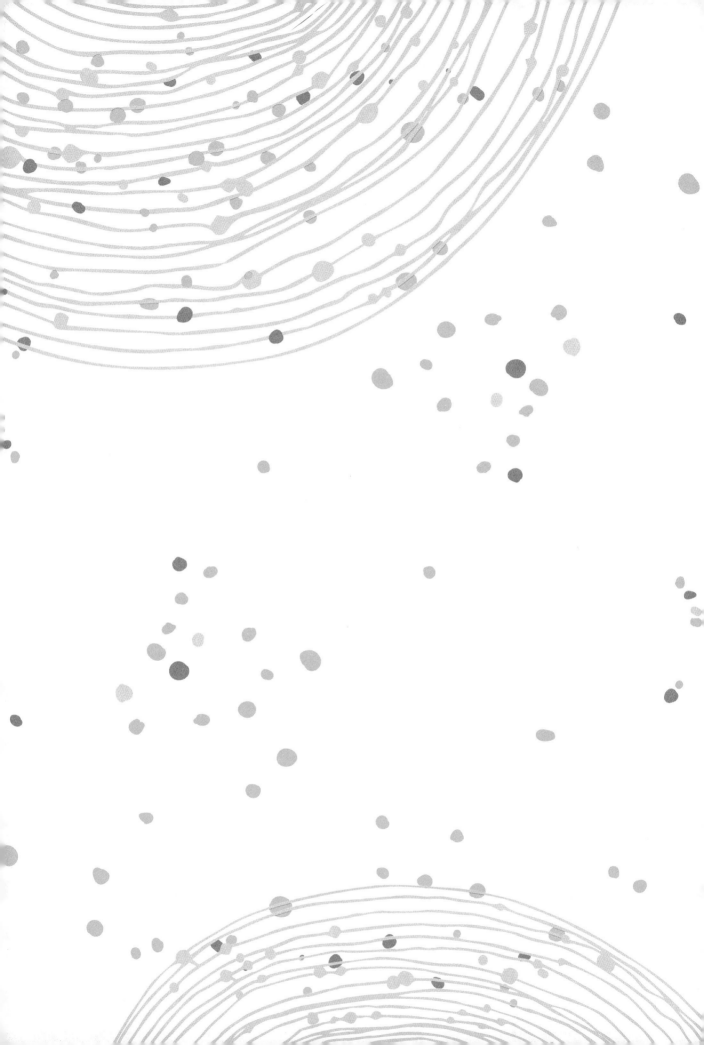

Apply: Sayings

Read the passage and answer the questions.

An old man went to visit his doctor because he was feeling under the weather. It was also time for his yearly check-up. At his doctor's appointment, the doctor suggested that he eat an apple a day to keep the doctor away. Rather than being confused, the man was encouraged by the doctor's advice. From that day forward, he decided to change his ways. The old man looked up healthy recipes and began cooking healthier meals. The old man also joined a gym to start exercising. Even though he was 75, he figured it was better late than never! With this new life, he began to meet new friends. They were active and healthy people, just like him. It was nice to find a group of people who shared the same interests as him. It reminded him that birds of a feather flock together.

1. Identify the sayings used in the passage and describe them using your own words.

Saying	Meaning

2. Draw a picture that illustrates at least 3 sayings used in the passage.

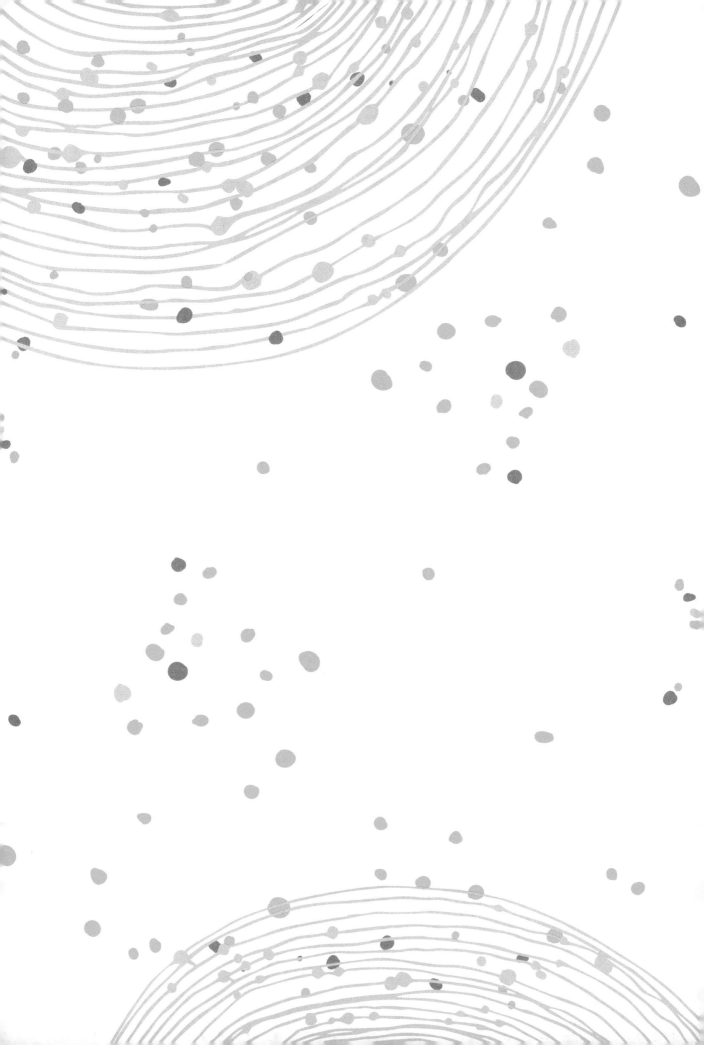

Glossary

academic word – a word used in educational settings more than in conversation; often a more precise word in place of a more common word

adage – an old, familiar saying that describes a common truth

adjective – a word that modifies, or describes, a noun or pronoun

affix – a word part attached to a root or base word to create a new word

alliteration – the use of words with the same or close to the same beginning sounds

allusion – a reference to a familiar literary or historical person or event, used to make an idea more easily understood

antonym – a word that means the opposite of another word

biography – the story of someone's life written by another person

book review – a piece of writing that gives an opinion about a book and tells about it

brainstorming – before writing, a way for the writer to come up with ideas

caption – text that tells more about an illustration, such as a photograph or other graphic

cause – the reason something happens

cause and effect – a situation in which one condition or fact, the cause, results in another, the effect

character – a person or animal in a story

character trait – a quality of a person or character; part of a personality

characterization – the techniques an author uses to reveal character traits; characters are revealed by their words, thoughts, actions, and what other characters say about them

chronological order – a way to organize that puts details in time order

claim – an idea or opinion presented, or a stand taken, in an argument

compare – to explain how two or more things are alike

compare-and-contrast organization – a structure for text that shows how two or more things are similar and different

complex sentence – a sentence that has one independent part and at least one dependent part

compound sentence – a sentence that has at least two independent parts

concluding sentence – the last sentence of a paragraph; it often summarizes the paragraph

conclusion – a decision made about something not stated, using information provided and what is already known

conclusion – the final paragraph of a written work

concrete – (adj.) real or physical; able to be perceived by the senses

conflict – a problem or issue that a character faces in a story

conjunction – a word used to join parts of a sentence, such as *and*, *but*, and *or*

consequence – what happens because of an action or event

context – the parts of a sentence or passage surrounding a word

context clue – a word or phrase in a text that helps you figure out the meaning of an unknown word

contrast – to explain how two or more things are different

coordinating conjunction – one of seven words—*and*, *but*, *for*, *nor*, *or*, *so*, *yet*—that connects words, phrases, or independent clauses

copyright – the right held by one person or company to publish, sell, distribute, and reproduce a work of art, literature, or music

correlative conjunction – one part of a pair of conjunctions that connects words or groups of words; example pairs: *either/or*, *neither/nor*, *both/and*

description – writing that uses words that show how something looks, sounds, feels, tastes, or smells
Example: The sky is a soft, powdery blue, and the golden sun feels warm on my face.

detail – a fact or description that tells more about a topic

diagram – a drawing or design that shows how pieces of information are related

dialect – a way of speaking that is particular to a certain group of people, place, or time

dialogue – the words that characters say in a written work

direct address – calling a person or animal by name or title; for example, "Look, Mary, I found it!" or "Doctor, come here."

direct quotation – the exact words of a speaker or writer

draft – an early effort at a piece of writing, not the finished work

drafting – of writing, the stage or step in which the writer first writes the piece

drama – another word for *play*

editorial – an article in a publication that gives an opinion held by its editor or editors; an opinion piece similar to such an article

effect – the result of a cause

evidence – a specific detail, such as a fact or expert opinion, that supports a reason

fact – something that can be proven true

figurative language – words that describe something by comparing it to something completely different
Example: Rain fell in buckets and the streets looked like rivers.

firsthand account – an account told from direct personal experience or observation

first-person narrator – a narrator who tells a story from the first-person point of view

first-person point of view – the telling of a story by a character in that story, using pronouns such as *I*, *me*, and *we*

formal language – the choice of words, phrases, and sentences that adhere to the conventional standards of grammar, usage, and mechanics

fragment – an incomplete sentence that begins with a capital letter and ends with a punctuation mark

free verse – poetry whose rhythm follows natural speech patterns and does not rely on regular rhyme or meter

future perfect tense – verb tense that shows an action that will be completed in the future before another action happens

future progressive tense – verb tense that shows an ongoing action that has not yet happened
Example: I will be swimming most days this summer.

glossary – a list of important terms and their meanings that is usually found in the back of a book

graph – a pictorial way to display data

graphic – a picture, photograph, map, diagram, or other image

graphic organizer – a visual device, such as a diagram or chart, that helps a writer plan a piece of writing

heading – a title within the body of a text that tells the reader something important about a section of the text

helping verb – a word that works with the main verb to show action; for example, *has, have, will, do, did, can*

historical fiction – a story set in a historical time period that includes facts about real people, places, and events, but also contains fictional elements that add dramatic interest to the story

homograph – a word that has the same spelling as another word but has a different pronunciation and meaning

homonym – a word that is spelled the same and sounds the same but has a different meaning from another word

homophone – a word that sounds the same as another word but has a different spelling and meaning

hook – a surprising idea or group of words used to grab the reader's attention, usually at the beginning of a work

idiom – a group of words that does not actually mean what it says
Examples: raining cats and dogs; a month of Sundays

imagery – language that helps readers imagine how something looks, sounds, smells, feels, or tastes

infer – to use clues and what you already know to make a guess

inference – a guess that readers make using the clues that an author gives them in a piece of writing

informal language – language that may include, for example, personal feeling, slang, contractions, humor, and fragments

informational essay – a kind of writing that informs or explains

informational text – text written to explain and give information on a topic

interjection – a word (or words) that expresses strong feeling

Internet – a global communications system of linked computer networks

introduction – the first paragraph of an essay, identifying the topic and stating the main idea

legend – a story that is passed down for many years to teach the values of a culture; a legend may or may not contain some true events or people

line – a row of words in a poem

main idea – the most important point the author makes; it may be stated or unstated

mass media – communication—such as television, movies, radio, and newspapers —designed to reach many, or the mass of, people

media – all the ways by which something can be shown, shared, or expressed

metaphor – a figure of speech that compares two unlike things, without using the word *like* or *as*
Example: The cat's eyes were emeralds shining in the night.

meter – the arrangement of words in poetry based on rhythm, accents, and the number of syllables in a line

mood – the emotions or feelings conveyed in a literary work

narrative – a kind of writing that tells a story

narrative nonfiction – a story based on fact, told using the same kind of plan and features that fictional stories use

narrative poem – a poem that tells a story

narrator – the teller of a story

nonfiction – writing that presents facts and information to explain, describe, or persuade; for example, newspaper articles and biographies are nonfiction

nuance – a very small difference in meaning

onomatopoeia – the use of words that show sounds, such as the words *moo*, *woof*, *quack*, *squash*

opinion – something that a person thinks or believes, but which cannot be proven to be true

outline – an organized list of topics in an essay

pace/pacing (in speech) – the speed, and the change of speeds, of a speaker's delivery

pace/pacing (in writing) – the speed at which events unfold or information is revealed in a narrative

paraphrase – to restate information in one's own words

past perfect tense – verb tense that shows an action that was completed before another action happened

past progressive tense – verb tense that shows an ongoing action that already happened
Example: I was sleeping earlier.

personal narrative – an essay about a personal experience of the writer

personification – giving human qualities to something that is not human
Example: The thunder shouted from the clouds.

perspective – the way someone sees the world

persuasive essay – an essay in which the writer tries to convince readers to agree with a stance on an issue

plagiarism – use of another person's words without giving that person credit as a source

plot – what happens in a story; the sequence of events

poem – a piece of poetry

point of view – the perspective a story is told from

precise language – language that is specific and exact

predicate – the verb or verb phrase in a sentence

prediction – a guess about what might happen that is based on information in a story and what you already know

prefix – a word part with its own meaning that can be added to the beginning of a base word or root to make a new word with a different meaning

preposition – a word that begins a phrase that ends with a noun or pronoun Examples: In the phrases "over the bridge" and "to me," the words *over* and *to* are prepositions.

prepositional phrase – a group of words that begins with a preposition and usually ends with the noun or a pronoun that is the object of the preposition

present perfect tense – verb tense that shows an action that either (1) happened at a vague time in the past or (2) started in the past and has continued into the present

present progressive tense – verb tense that shows an ongoing action that is happening now Example: I am eating breakfast right now.

prewriting – the stage or step of writing in which a writer chooses a topic, gathers ideas, and plans what to write

primary source – a record made by a person who saw or took part in an event or who lived at the time

problem (literature) – an issue a character must solve in a story

problem-solution structure (writing) – organizational pattern in which a problem is described, followed by descriptions of its solution or possible solutions

proofreading – the stage or step of the writing process in which the writer checks for errors in grammar, punctuation, capitalization, and spelling

proper adjective – an adjective form of a proper noun; for example, *European* or *Japanese*

proper noun – a noun that names a particular person, place, thing, or idea

prose – the form of written language without the rhyme, rhythm, and meter that the language of poetry has

proverb – a brief, popular saying that describes a wise thought

publishing – the stage or step of the writing process in which the writer makes a clean copy of the piece and shares it

reason – a statement that explains why something is or why it should be

relative adverb – one of the three adverbs *when*, *where*, and *why* that relates an adjective clause to the noun or pronoun the clause describes

relative pronoun – a pronoun that relates an adjective clause to the noun or pronoun the clause describes

repetition – repeating words or phrases

research – to find information through study rather than through personal experience

resolution – the outcome of a story

revising – the stage or step of the writing process in which the writer rereads and edits the draft, correcting errors and making changes in content or organization that improve the piece

rhyme – the use of words that end with the same sounds; for example, *cat* and *hat* rhyme

rhyme scheme – the pattern of rhymes made by the last sounds in the lines of a poem, shown by a different letter of the alphabet to represent each rhyme

rhythm (poetry) – a regular pattern of sound and beats within a poem

root – a word part with a special meaning to which prefixes and suffixes can be added; for example, *spec* is a root that means "see"

run-on – two or more sentences that have been joined without a conjunction or proper punctuation

scene (drama) – a subdivision of an act of a play that happens at a fixed time and place

scientific method – a way to find answers by experimenting, observing, and drawing conclusions

secondary source – a record made by a person who did not see or take part in an event, or who made the record later

secondhand account – an account told through research rather than by way of direct personal experience or observation

sensory detail – descriptive detail that appeals to any of the senses—sight, hearing, touch, smell, or taste

sensory language – language that appeals to the five senses

sentence – a group of words that tells a complete thought

sequence – the order in which things happen

sequence of events (plot) – what happens in a story; the plot

setting – where and when a literary work takes place

simile – a comparison between two things using the words *like* or *as*
Example: I didn't hear him come in because he was as quiet as a mouse.

simple sentence – a sentence that is one independent clause

source – a provider of information; a book, a historical document, online materials, and an interviewee are all sources

speaker – the imaginary person who speaks the words of a poem, not the poet

stage directions – instructions from a playwright that tell the actors what to do during the play

stanza – a group of lines in a poem

structure (writing) – the way a piece of writing is organized

style – the words a writer chooses and the way the writer arranges the words into sentences

subject – a word or words that tell whom or what the sentence is about

subordinating conjunction – a word that is used to introduce a dependent clause

suffix – a word part added to the end of a base word or root that changes the meaning or part of speech of a word

summarize (informational text) – to restate briefly the main points of a text

summarize (literary text: story, play, poem) – to tell in order the most important ideas or events of a text

summary – a short retelling that includes only the most important ideas or events of a text

supporting detail – a detail that gives more information about a main idea

suspense – uncertainty about what will happen

syllable – a unit of spoken language; a syllable contains only one vowel sound

synonym – a word that means the same, or almost the same, as another word

tag question – a question, or tag, added to a statement to engage the listener; for example: It's nice out, isn't it?

text feature – part of a text that helps a reader locate information and determine what is most important; some examples are the title, table of contents, headings, pictures, and glossary

theme – the author's message or big idea

thesis statement – the sentence that states the main idea of an essay

third-person point of view – the telling of a story by someone outside of the action, using the third-person pronouns *he*, *she*, and *they*

time order (sequential) organizational structure – the arrangement of ideas according to when they happened

tone (literature) – the author's feelings toward the subject or characters of a text

tone (speaking) – a speaker's attitude as shown by his or her voice

topic – the subject of a text

topic sentence – the sentence that expresses the main idea of a paragraph

transition – a word, phrase, or clause that connects ideas

transitional word or phrase – a word or phrase, such as *for example*, used to move from one idea to another

viewpoint (related to point of view) – the perspective of a person or group

visual (n.) – a graphic, picture, or photograph

visualization – the picturing of something in one's mind

visualize – to picture things in your mind as you read

website – a place on the Internet devoted to a specific organization, group, or individual

writing prompt – a sentence or sentences that ask for a particular kind of writing

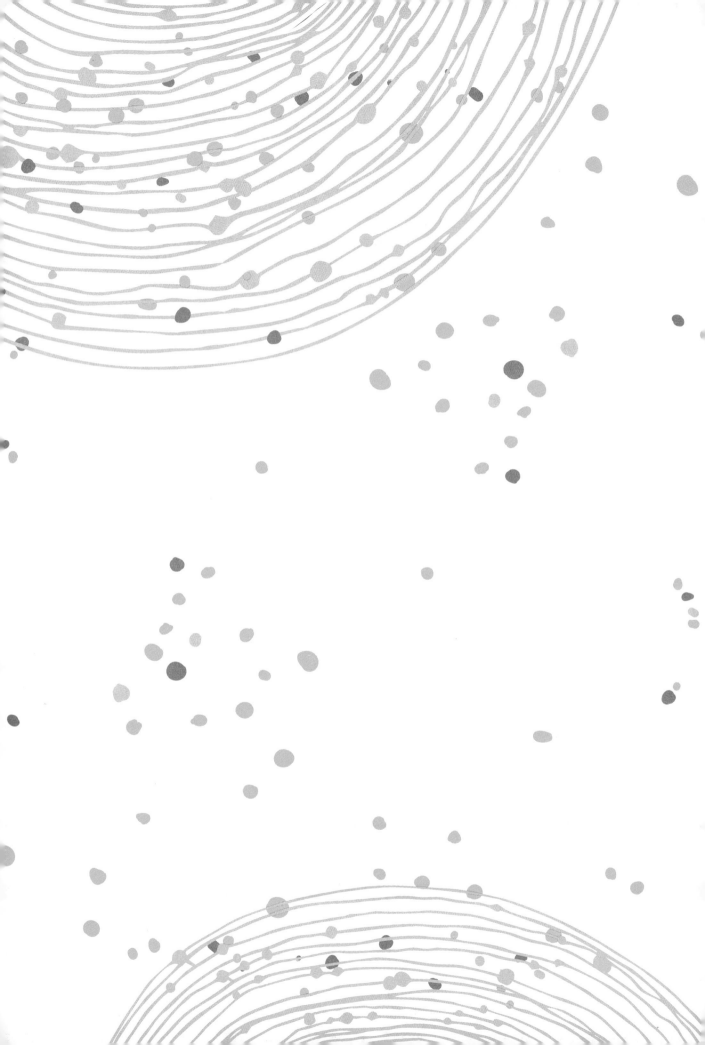